CHOOSE HER EVERY DAY (OR LEAVE HER)

Bryan Withrow Reeves

Experience Bryan's Life Coaching and
Relationship Coaching Programs at

www.BryanReeves.com

Cover Art by Akira Chan akirachan.com
Cover Design by Paul Preston
Layout and Typesetting by Michel Khalil

PART 1 – PREPARATION

PART 2 – DANCING IN THE FIRE

PART 3 – TRANSCENDING THE FIRE

INTRODUCTION

"We are so connected the word 'connected' doesn't even make sense."
– Rumi

For over thirty years I've been tenaciously throwing myself into the transformational fires of intimate relationship over and over again. For I began a romantic, believing in the popular songs and fairytale movies of my 1980s youth that all promised a beautiful princess was waiting for me just beyond some horizon. Whitney Houston swore she was saving all her love for me, and John Cusack (in "Say Anything") assured me I'd win over a woman's heart by just being nice to her.

When my romantic escapades with women began in my early teens, I was certain love would be easy. Besides, I got along great with my three sisters and two moms (mom, step-mom), so I figured that if anyone should excel at loving a woman that someone should be me.

What I actually experienced over the next twenty years proved dramatically otherwise.

In my early 20s I became an Air Force Officer tasked with managing billion-dollar avionics programs and launching GPS satellites into space. The military also afforded me the opportunity to earn a Masters Degree in Human Relations. Yet none of that responsibility or education taught me anything about how to relate well to a woman in intimacy.

After my service ended at age 26, I became a personal growth workshop junkie. I threw myself into all kinds of so-called "transformational exercises," from questioning my stressful thoughts to loudly howling out my painful past to eye-gazing deep into the eye-ball souls of countless willing women (and men, too). Yet still I could never understand why women always seemed to want more from me when I believed I was already giving her so much.

I was also a long-time practitioner of spiritual disciplines and mindfulness meditation. Various teachers and practices had taught me an abundance of big, liberating ideas about life, about myself, but none offered any useful insight into why I kept choosing women so easily angered by me. Nor did any spiritual practice ever help stop me from (recklessly) fighting a woman's anger with mine.

Indeed, despite all my best intentions and efforts, I just couldn't succeed at a relationship with a woman.

By the time I was 36, all I saw around and behind me was the twisted and hideous wreckage of dozens of relationships that had come crashing spectacularly down from their high-heaven hopes. Rather than see my part in things and really learn from my mistakes, I mostly just blamed my sweet-smelling co-pilots for foolishly flipping whatever knobs and hysterically yanking at the steering wheel such that she made our fiery demise inevitable. It never occurred to me that I might be the one who needed flying lessons.

It was then, at 36, amidst the blazing wreckage of yet another catastrophic heartbreak, that I resolved to stop sucking at love. I refused to believe I was destined to screw up relationships for the rest of my life. I decided there must be secrets to love and intimacy that someone could teach me – that someone should have taught me 20 years earlier.

It is true that when the student is ready, the teacher appears. Because I was truly ready to do love well, whatever that required of me, and so my teachers of exquisite relationship began to appear.

Soon after this declaration a friend put a book into my hands: The Way Of The Superior Man (David Deida). I drank it down like a sun-burnt man who's been wandering lost in the desert drinks down his first cup of cold water. All of a sudden I felt like Neo in The Matrix awakening to see the world anew! Where I once saw people, movies, trees, cities, music, art, sports, and sunsets, as relatively firm objects or things or interesting experiences to be had or figured out, I now saw undulating expressions of Masculine and Feminine energies dancing together in the moment-by-moment unfolding of Life, itself.

My learning and growth accelerated from there.

Living in Los Angeles – after migrating across the country from Miami with a spiritual music band I'd managed for five years – I had access to world class teachers. I began to attend intimacy and attraction workshops in Santa Monica with Michaela Boehm (now famously known as the "intimacy coach to the stars"). Michaela taught me many things, including how to be a still, rooted, openhearted expression of Masculine presence in service to the dynamic, ever-changing dance of Feminine flow. I got to go head-to-head on stage with Dr. Pat Allen, the feisty 80-yrs-aged author of Getting To 'I Do', during her weekly relationship talks (she called them "shows") at a tiny Odyssey Theater in west LA. She would invite people on stage to talk with her about their relationship challenges, and I took advantage of the opportunity. Our conversations were sometimes adversarial, often hilarious, and always educational.

Surrounded as I was by the sexually adventurous culture of southern California, I also gingerly dipped my genitals into the realms of sexual tantra. I learned breathing practices to help my body feel more "orgasmic" while holding off ejaculation.

I experienced all this and more, starving as I was for teachers and adventures that might unlock the secrets of love and intimacy.

I also dated and dated and dated, intentionally practicing what I was learning on dates, and with female friends, too. For example, an ex-girlfriend once complained that I wouldn't walk on the street-side of the sidewalk with her. At the time I saw her complaint as arbitrary and absurd. But as I learned what it meant to offer masculine presence to a woman, and what impact it had on her, I started experimenting with it. I immediately noticed two things profound: One, I felt viscerally stronger in my body, as if my spine was suddenly plugged into an electric socket. Two, I noticed that in the moment I moved my body to be street-side of her, every woman's body showed subtle signs of relaxing – whether a sudden deep sigh or a hint of delight escaping her face.

I'd never been tuned into such subtleties in the body before or understood any differences between masculine and feminine communication. I was giddy to be finally learning what I should have been taught years ago.

My journey of spiritual awakening began when I was ten. But it wasn't until I was 36, and had suffered immensely, that my journey of "relational awakening" began. I'm now 46 and five years into the extraordinary relationship I ached a lifetime for. I didn't get here by accident. I got here by finally accepting I didn't know what I was doing, and by being willing to learn.

This book is the collection of essays I wrote throughout this 7 years journey to discover the secrets of intimacy, relationship, love. It contains many of the insights, wisdoms, and practices that I now teach my coaching clients, both individuals and couples, and certainly continue to use in my own relationship. This is by no means complete as my awakening journey remains ever-unfolding. I also do not insist everything here is absolute truth (or that any of it is), or that my insights and discoveries are applicable to everyone. I always reserve the right to be wrong.

Do know this: If you're doing it well, the journey into intimacy with another is a courageous journey into intimacy with your own true self.

HOW TO READ THIS BOOK

There is no wrong or right way to read this book. You can start at the beginning, or with whichever chapter speaks to your heart and jump around from there. These chapters are not necessarily in chronological order, and each one stands alone a fully contained story or insight. Some have actual practices you can try; some will simply serve to inspire your own thoughts and awareness.

Should you choose to start at the beginning and read through to the end, you will be witness to a man's evolutionary journey in understanding and experiencing of relationship, intimacy, love. At the beginning, I'm single, still recovering from a painful breakup while beginning to wake up and not yet a practicing relationship coach. Somewhere in the middle I meet a special woman. By the end I'm five years into committed relationship with that woman, and now a thriving life and relationship coach working with individuals and couples all over the world.

A NOTE ON GENDER

In this book, when I say "masculine" I do not mean "man," and when I say "feminine" I do not mean "woman." Every human, whatever their gender-identification or sexual orientation, has both feminine and masculine potentials. I hold it would do humanity well that we each work to cultivate our capacities to fully offer whichever expressions of masculine or feminine being would serve in any given moment.

Still, I must acknowledge that I identify as a predominantly heterosexual man and have written many of these essays much like journalistic reports of my own personal experiences. If you do not identify as heterosexual, although I implore you not to take my gender-frames literally and instead see the deeper patterns underneath, I recognize it may at times be difficult for you to do so. With deep reverence for your experience, I leave this for you to navigate.

ACKNOWLEDGEMENTS

Finally, I must acknowledge all my teachers who have over many years helped stretch open my mind to deeper understandings of the world, of others, and of myself, such that my own yearning heart has and continues to become ever more present and alive to the absolute majesty and wonder of life, and of love.

I encourage you to explore the work of these people who have profoundly influenced my own work, and the depth and quality of my life. If you listen with a knowing heart, you will hear the ripples and echoes of their contributions to humanity reverberating throughout my own: Clarissa Pinkola Estes, David Deida, Michaela Boehm, Steve James, Terry Real, Esther Perel, Robert Moore, Douglass Gillete, Robert Johnson, Robert Bly, Dr. Pat Allen, Stan Tatkin, Robert Duggan, Dianne Connelly, Ash Ruiz, Grandmother Ayahuasca, Byron Katie, Abraham Esther-Hicks, Eckhart Tolle, Mark Twain, Bill Plotnick, Michael Meade, Carlos Castaneda, Joseph Campbell, John O'Donahue, Anthony Robbins, Ilonka Harezi, Rev James Trapp, Michael Beckwith, Marianne Williamson, Psilocybin Mushrooms, Rainer Maria Rilke, Alan Watts, and countless others.

I appreciate my dear friends, Brandi, Jason, and Tait, for helping me make some difficult decisions about what to keep in this collection of essays, and what to keep out; and Gina, my Client Relations Manager, who helps me spend less time in my manager-mind and more time in my creative-heart.

I also want to acknowledge my Lady Silvy Khoucasian. Without her, I would only have good ideas. With her, and in many ways because of her, I am living the life I always dreamed of. As my intimate life partner, she is both my great destroyer of good ideas (so that more useful ones may emerge) and my greatest teacher of actually living real love and courageous intimacy.

PART 1

PREPARATION

— 1 —

NO ONE EVER TAUGHT ME HOW TO BE A MAN

No one ever taught me how to be a Man.

I love my two fathers, my dad and step-dad. I'm truly blessed to have both of these good men in my life. But it was my two mothers (mom and step-mom) who were the strong, orienting leaders in my early life, who held the families together and made sure I always knew everything would be ok.

My dads ... well, I never felt them fully present for me. As I look back, I see my moms holding the world together while my two dads seemed to mostly just be holding on for dear life – and mostly to their wives, my mothers.

But I didn't only grow up with disoriented fathers. Just like you, I was (and still am) immersed in a world dominated by warped, immature expressions of manhood and masculinity:

- *Constantly sexualizing women.*
- *Ridiculing vulnerability.*
- *Woman-magnet, gun-toting hero-worship.*
- *Homophobia.*
- *Power-focused blame-game government politics.*
- *Bullying from every angle.*
- *A win-at-all-costs / winner-take-all competitive ethos.*
- *Anti-feminine misogyny of infinite variety.*

Even the offensive words I learned to use as a young boy to assert dominance: bitch, fag, crybaby, nancy-boy, cocksucker, motherfucker. All insults that strike their blow by chopping down the Feminine. My personal favorite is "pussy." I figure anything that references the wonder of a woman's capacity for yielding life should be reserved for only the highest of praise. Yet it's merely a tool for insult. … us and our misogynistic genital shame.

Generations of western men are in crisis. And we have no idea how to step up with a mature masculinity in our relationships with women. At 39, I'm only now discovering what this immature masculine ethos has cost me and the women I've been in relationship with.

I've demeaned my female partners by treating them as emotionally-flawed versions of men. I've run away from them, fed up and disgusted, when they only needed me to stand fast and love them deeply. I've lied because I thought their weaker sensitivities couldn't handle difficult truth (little did I know I was the one who couldn't handle it). I've used their bodies for my pleasure and then disappeared quick as I came, so to speak.

I've failed my more core-feminine partners in countless heartbreaking ways because no one ever taught me how to be a Man. I don't mean in traditional ways like paying for everything or being the one to get the car fixed or opening doors. I don't believe in such fixed and firm rules. I simply mean that no one ever taught me how to show up fully present … as … a … Man.

I see so much of it now. My heart still breaks as I look backwards and see the awful wake of female wreckage I created in years past. Sure, they had their own growing up to do. Let me not condescend now by suggesting that I – a man – was solely responsible for the experiences of these "poor girls." Of course not. That's just more clever self-righteous misogyny in disguise. Nonetheless, I see so clearly how I failed to show up for the women in my life, over and over and over.

Boys today are still in crisis. They commit suicide at a higher rate than girls. They feel isolated and angry. They're the ones shooting up schools and concerts. Our girls are in crisis, too. Indeed, the world is confused as ever.

As we continue to infuse a new generation of boys and girls with the same stunted-growth versions of masculinity and femininity, we remain disconnected from the profound gifts of our wondrous human essence.

Fortunately, we're collectively grow ever more wise to this tragic deception. I'm certainly seeing it. As I near my 40th birthday, the mature Masculine man in me is awakening. What I'm discovering is not only massive appreciation for the mysterious and untamable Feminine essence in a woman, but also for that same wild Feminine essence in me, too.

What's more, as the MAN inside me awakens more and more every day, my life's work transforms. Which is the most exciting thing about overcoming the "absence of father" and finally learning what it actually means to be a heart-centered, genuinely powerful, authentic Man in the world. As I continue to do my inner healing work and overcome the overwhelming absence of father, I'm awakening to an authentic life purpose that finally makes life truly worth living.

Still, how different life would have been had a wise elder man long ago shown me the way.

 2

A MAN'S EVOLUTION
IN INTIMACY WITH WOMEN

I used to just want a woman's sexy body. Later I wanted her intelligent mind, too. Now, as the mature masculine man in me awakens, there's something far more precious than her body or even her mind that I covet: *her devotional heart.*

Here's my evolution in intimacy with women:

As a teenager, sex dominated my mind, and a warm smooth body could easily satisfy. Didn't matter what thoughts she thought or how deep her connection to heart. The depth of my curiosity literally stopped at skin deep.

All I cared about was, What does her skin feel like against mine? What does she smell like? Taste like? Will she press herself passionately up against me? Will she moan? Will she scratch me, bite me, tease me? Will she stick her wet tongue in my ear? And where in the world of her body is that magic little hidden spot I've heard so much about that's supposed to make her heavens shake? What will happen when our bodies meet?

These were the sensual if shallow depths of my interest in the feminine form as a young man.

The first stage is purely focused on the physical body.

This first stage of body-focus persisted throughout my 20s well into my 30s. Many people in our culture live primarily in this first stage throughout their lives. Many more core-masculine men remain stuck on female body infatuation long after their own bodies can even do anything about it. For some core-feminine women, however, their first-stage focus may be less about a man's physical body and more about his "body" of material resources. Lest you think this sexist, you may consider that a man experiencing this first-stage of intimate relating won't really care about a woman's access to resources, and a first-stage woman can be easily influenced by a man's.

For my part, I remember struggling in this first stage with my attraction to an early girlfriend when her body began to change from sexy lithe teenager to a more curvaceous young woman. She was an amazing young lady, but as her body changed I lost interest in her – a first-stage reaction.

As my 30s wore on, what a woman thought about started to become far more interesting to me. Who she was in conversation began to matter more. Shallow-minded sexy chics (at least as my arrogance perceived them to be shallow-minded) became less attractive. I started longing for thought-provoking sexy chics, the ones who could parry with me in conversation and perhaps teach me things about the world I didn't already know. I was still primarily body-focused, but I began to more fully appreciate a woman who could meet me intellectually. I wanted to make love to a woman's mind almost as much as her body.

This second stage is mind-body focused.

If you're reading this, you likely live mostly in this stage. You may surely still experience body-focus temptations, but your attraction to mind complements if not overrides most physical attractions. It could be also that a more feminine person experiences this differently than a more masculine person. A more Masculine person tends to relate (connect) to the world more through the mind-intellect filter, whereas a more feminine person tends to relate (connect) more through feeling experiences.

Many people can fake this second-stage experience, at least for a time. After all, "you're shallow" is no compliment in our world. But when a first-stage person who is pretending (even if unconsciously so) to be a second-stage person has a partner who loses physical allure or substantial material resources, the eyes and libido of that first-stage consciousness will start wandering.

Interestingly, I found over and over in this second-stage era that there was no woman who's mind I could ever fully embrace. I would inevitably encounter something in her thought-world that I would object to: she's not ambitious enough, worldly enough, kind enough, philosophical enough, smart enough ... whatever. She was never enough. These objections would invariably diminish my capacity for true intimacy with her.

How could I fully be with her when I was resisting how she was being?

Despite that enduring obstacle, my second-stage orientation held that loving a woman complete meant loving her "mind and body." I was sure this orientation would yield the magic formula for fairytale love.

Alas, there was another stage yet to come – a third stage. I'm only now waking up to this third stage, and I'm profoundly hungry for it.

This third stage is body-mind-spirit focused.

It's about Devotion. While it certainly encompasses attraction to body and mind, it also transcends them. I'm not going to pretend to know the experience just yet, for I can't say I've ever been truly devoted to a woman. Yet.

I am noticing that as a more mature masculine essence begins to stir in me, an attractive body and mind alone no longer suffice. I want more than just to intertwine myself with her physical and mental worlds; I want to penetrate the depths of her soul. I want not just a warm body and intellectual play, I want her deep devotional heart.

I also want to give her mine.

While I'm still learning what this means, what I do know is I have finally evolved to a moment in life where my deepest yearning is for the experience of such complete devotion to the Feminine that my Love both embraces her body and mind but also transcends them.

However, I currently have no feminine partner to engage on this adventure. And there are certainly days when I taste the pungent angst of this yearning as yet unrequited. Sometimes it feels like reaching desperate for a breath underwater.

But let's see where Life wants to take this.

I'm ready for stage three, so says the awakening man in me.

"Love is freedom, but not total. If love becomes devotion, then it becomes total freedom. It means surrendering yourself completely."

– Osho

 3

MEN AREN'T SUPPOSED TO UNDERSTAND WOMEN

I've finally realized that I'm not supposed to understand my woman. I am only supposed to love her in all her wild mystery.

I wouldn't want to ever completely understand a woman, anyway. Like most men, once I understand or completely figure something out (or even think I have) I grow bored of it, hungry for a next challenge.

Recently, I freebased every Mount Everest documentary on Netflix. I was stunned by how many male climbers, soon after their moment of sweet imperious glory standing above everyone else on the planet, immediately started dreaming of doing it again – though with some added twist to make it harder next time, like refusing bottled oxygen or taking a route known to kill even more men. (Everest kills 1 in 40 who attempt to climb it … and that's on the easy route).

To stop pushing at the edges of what is possible is like death to masculine being.

A more feminine-core woman is the spiritual Mount Everest for a more masculine-core man (and for a more masculine-core woman, too).

He shouldn't hope to ever truly conquer her (or even think he has).

For what then? Boredom is what then.

We challenge-hungry men need to learn to honor this great mystery that is a woman.

There is a reason masculine men (and more masculine-identified women) are drawn to the raw wilds in nature. It is where we know instinctively we can go to shake off our petty little ego selves that rob us of our life force like pick-pocket thieves in the city subway. The immensity of nature overwhelms that small self so we can connect with the deep stillness of eternity, and stillness is the essential nature of our masculine energy.

Yet the wilds of nature also challenge us. A man's sense of worthiness is largely derived from his ability to rise, meet, and ultimately overcome any force that would otherwise destroy him. Like the intense emotions often easily conjured up by many women, the raw forces of nature can draw a man to rise up in every way.

One of the most thrilling moments in my life happened on a stormy autumn night at my parents' backwoods home when I was a teenager. A nasty torrential downpour was threatening to burst the leaf-clogged gutters hanging precariously from our roof when my step-father looked stern at me and said, "Let's go."

After donning slick rain coats and grabbing a rickety metal ladder from the garage, we stepped face first outside into a cold sideways rain. Clawing our way up the slippery ladder, we rounded our bodies onto a roof much steeper and more precarious than it looked from the ground, which suddenly felt so far beneath my feet that I had to fight off a sickening nausea. The winds howled all around us, thunder boomed above, and countless pellets of rain pelted me from every angle. My mom and sisters watched from inside, safe, warm, huddled together, framed and glowing in the light of the living room window. I bent dangerously towards the edge railings, careful not to lose my balance.

As I scooped out thick muddy clumps of wet leaves and twisted branches, tossing them to the muddy earth far below, I had one delighted thought: "THIS IS FUCKING AWESOME!!!"

There's just something profoundly satisfying about taking on the wild, regardless of whether I even live to tell about it (though that is always preferable). This is why the masculine creature delights at slashing his way through wild forests, scaling treacherous mountain trails, and sailing across vast oceans that in one moment may bathe him serene like a king in golden moonlight and in the next unleash a rage that dumps him overboard like rotting refuse.

Wild is the nature of the Feminine. She drives mad the mortal man full of arrogance in believing he could ever conquer her.

"What is the Wild Woman?" writes Clarissa Pinkola Estes in her masterpiece, <u>Women Who Run With The Wolves</u>:

"She is the female soul.... She is the source of the feminine. She is all that is of instinct, of the worlds both seen and hidden.... She encourages humans to remain multilingual; fluent in the languages of dreams, passion, and poetry. She whispers from night dreams .... She is ideas, feelings, urges, and memory. She has been lost and half forgotten for a long, long time. She is the source, the light, the night, the dark, and daybreak. She is the smell of good mud and the back leg of the fox. The birds which tell us secrets belong to her. She is the voice that says, "This way, this way."

Men, I pray you learn to appreciate, as I am still learning to appreciate, that our women are not crazy. Not even the craziest of them.

We tend to think of a woman as something that should make logical sense to our brains. When she doesn't, rather than revel in her alluring mystery, we wave her off with a hairy hand and call her crazy, high-maintenance, stupid, illogical, weak, emotional, unstable. Or we blame our overwhelm on her PMS.

We've grown up fearful of the feminine nature because we don't understand it. And never will. We're not supposed to. The feminine essence of being is by its nature unbound by any reason or logic that could possibly contain it.

We demean the feminine, and women, with everyday misogynistic slang that we men often sling at each other without even noticing: pussy, bitch, cocksucker, motherfucker, whore. I've done it my whole life. I still sometimes catch myself.

Our fear of the feminine has made us men who recoil when a woman cries. Her tears don't make sense to us. Her tears often don't make sense to her, either. We think logically and want to fix the problem we understand. But what she's saying is wrong isn't what's actually wrong. Even if it is, it's not often a technical solution she's after. And we know this because solving her problem our way rarely resolves her discontent. Which drives us mad. Her logic mocks ours.

Fortunately, I'm learning that our women don't need us to actually understand them, anyway. They know our compartmentalizing man-brains couldn't possibly grasp their true complexity.

What women need from us is our strong, mature, unwavering masculine presence; that deep, reassuring look in our eyes and a confident stance in our bodies that silently speaks our masculine vow: *"I've got you. I'm here. It's going to be ok. I love you."*

The only thing we need to understand is that a woman is not a defective version of a man.

She is our spiritual Mount Everest. If we are worthy and approach her with awe and humility, respecting her mystery, she will yield to us the most exquisite vistas of beauty and wonder. But if we underestimate and think we can conquer her, she'll freeze us in our trekking boots and flick us off her flanks like a snow tick.

Men, remember: It's not our job to understand women. It is our sacred duty to simply love them.

4

EMBRACING THE
ACHE OF LONELINESS

This is dedicated to the lonely. Even the lonely who have partners.

Have you ever felt *really* lonely?

I mean that kind of loneliness where you lie awake at night and your chest pulses with soft ache and your heart slowly burns as some persistent thought insists you're destined to go through this lifetime alone, that you're never going to find The One – or even anyone – in whose loving arms you'll finally experience … Home?

One late autumn many years ago, I was canoeing in the Canadian North Woods when I heard a faraway loon's evocative cry float despondent across the still, dark surface of a vast lake. The haunting sound of its longing sank into me like winter sadness. I've never forgotten it.

It's the sound my heart whispers out through my chest when I feel my aloneness severe.

Have you ever experienced this kind of loneliness?

You might have experienced it lying next to someone. Maybe even your husband or wife. That kind of loneliness can be torture. To be so close to a bliss that refuses to let you in.

We've all felt such deep loneliness, regardless how or to what degree. It's a byproduct of the human experience called "separate." I've felt it plenty. Both alone and in bed with my partner. I felt it last night, alone. It visits me for various reasons.

For years I've distracted myself from facing whatever that ache really is by pursuing unhealthy relationships, engaging in empty flings and empty promises, desperate online dating, medicinal masturbation and eating sugar … lots and lots of sugar. I've made girlfriends responsible for fixing it once and for all. As mere mortals who don't have such powers, I would blame them when it showed up again. I've also drowned myself with work, arrogance, porn, denial, even spiritual seeking; all so that I would have neither time nor energy to acknowledge its gnawing presence.

Since last summer, though, I've been cutting out most of that behavior (except a lot of that sugar). As I discover ever more what it means to honor my life as a more core-masculine Man, I realize I must turn into and face this loneliness that stalks me like death, and that I can trace back to my earliest memories. Not to conquer it, but to embrace it and explore whatever wisdom must lie beneath its menacing mask.

To feel the pain of loneliness, is to feel death's embrace.

So I have decided to get intimate with it, to invite it in and ask it questions. I want to know it. Not every day all the time, for I far more enjoy being my enthusiastic playful self. But when it clearly wants to come in, I allow it.

When it shows up, as it did last night, I breathe with it. I ask what it believes. This is what it tells me: *"I'm unlovable. Not good enough. Unworthy. Forever separate from everyone else, from Life, itself. Therefore no one will ever truly touch or know my true heart. I'm destined to be alone for all my days, and there's nothing to do about it."*

Ouch.

Intellectually, I know it's insane, this reclusive pain. Though it might be right about the last part. I might be destined to live out my days alone. How can I know?

Anyway, I just breathe with it. I give my chest freely to this ache and let it weep without trying to make it go away. I even agree with it, thinking silently, *"Ok, fine, so this is basically how it's always going to be. Me, alone in bed at night and through my days. Forever. So be it."*

And I let it cry.

I watch this passing weather; feel it soaking me through to my bones. I breathe.

Within a short time, a few minutes, it dissipates like a dark storm cloud that has shed all its rain. The sun may not immediately return, but the ache settles and I feel my body whole again.

I notice I'm cozy in my warm bed, deeply grateful for the life I got to live today. I think of all the amazing friends I have and the brilliant, beautiful women I've been fortunate to know and experience love with in this lifetime.

At this point, even though I'm alone, my hope will often flicker as the sweet-tasting thought quickly returns that there must be a good woman on this planet right now dreaming up someone just like me.

Even through my doubting, I can feel her presence. And when she shows up, I think to myself, this ache will surely never return. Of course, I know better now, so I remind myself that it probably WILL return in a moment of sudden disconnect and fear. Such moments happen. In partnership and without.

Hopefully, facing and embracing this loneliness now will help me breathe into it then and not make it anyone's fault. After all, it's just weather passing. Insane weather, perhaps. Still just weather.

Then, as I lay thoughtful and alone in my bed, my awareness quickly fading, I turn excitedly towards my nighttime Dream-Team, curious to experience whatever epic adventures they've prepared for me this night. They never let me down.

And I sleep.

"If you want to get rid of something, you must first allow it to flourish."
– Byron Katie

5

HEALING SOMETIMES MEANS LEARNING TO LIVE IN PEACE WITH THE PAIN

I'm discovering that sometimes healing just means learning to live in peace with the pain.

I've been to countless personal-growth workshops. I've questioned my stressful thoughts and limiting belief systems for days on end and accumulated countless hours of stranger eyegazing to weepy Whitney Houston songs. I've sat still and starving on desolate mountainsides while determined to reframe disappointments and disillusionment as profound blessings. I've danced in authentic celebration on many a dark cloud's silver lining, recited endless forgiveness mantras, lovingly held my phantom inner child and even walked (quickly) across 2000-degree glowing hot coals while screaming "YES! YES! YES!" all to prove just how much in control of my thoughts and perceptions I am.

I've done it all. Most of it, anyway.

Yet despite all the inner work I've done and all the beautiful insights my mind and heart are fortunate to see, there are some sorrows from my past that just never seem to fully exhaust their sadness.

Yes, certain ones do get easier to bear with time, and perhaps someday I'll be completely healed when I finally discover the right technique or some flash of divine insight startles me awake in bed. Or maybe I'll just eventually notice the wound no longer aches when life pokes its meddling, sharp-nailed fingers at it.

For now, though, simply making peace with the pain seems to be the best healing I can hope for. It might even be the very salvation my sadness so deeply longs for.

"I have been running so sweaty my whole life, urgent for a finish line. And I have been missing the rapture this whole time of being forever incomplete."
– Alanis Morissette

 6

6 REASONS WHY MEN MUST GIVE UP PORNOGRAPHY

"If you have the Internet, you have pornography in your home.
– Jill Manning, Ph.D., Marriage and Family Therapist

Author's note: I do not promote sexual shame or banning porn. This is simply an invitation to explore how online pornography can affect the experience and expression of a man's sexuality.

In my boyhood teenage days of yore, using pornography required patience, imagination.

One of my early adventures with porn occurred on weekday afternoons when I got home from middle school. Before anyone else arrived, I would sneak into my parents' bedroom closet with a small foot stool. I have no idea how I first found it, but resting atop the center ceiling panel, just inches from my horny little brain, was my step-father's erotic treasure trove of betamax video tapes with titles like "The Oriental Babysitter" and "Taxi Girls." I'd pop one into the black betamax box, hit play, and kick back on the lounger as sounds and images of ecstasy flooded my lusty synapses while I enjoyed myself a dozen or so times (oh, to be a teenager again).

A few years later, during high school, my tastes grew more sophisticated when mom started getting Victoria's Secret catalogs in the mail. Although I kinda already knew what the big secret was, these glossy mags made my imagination work harder at unlocking it each time, and I delighted in that. But a new catalog once every few weeks was far too infrequent for my insatiable teenage libido, and I could barely wait for the spring issues when lithe Victoria's would return to wearing sexy sundresses and seductive short skirts.

Those days of porn patience and teasing my imagination are gone.

At this very moment, I – and most every other man in Western Civilization – have in my hands a little device loaded with the entire known universe of pornographic material ready to stir my lust and blow my loins wide open. I never have to wait till Spring again.

"Enough is Enough" and "CovenantEyes," two internet safety organizations, offer these sobering statistics (note: CovenantEyes is Catholic-based; I am not):

- Every second, 28,258 Internet users are viewing pornography.
- American children begin viewing pornography at an average age of 11.
- The pornography industry is a $97 billion industry worldwide.
- Men are 543% more likely to look at porn than are women.
- More than 1 in 5 searches are for pornography on mobile devices.

Porn is ubiquitous. You might be surprised who uses online porn.

I have amazing male friends, attractive, dynamic, successful who've spent countless hours over many years caught in the sticky pornographic web. You would never imagine these men using online porn. But they have. And do. I have also used it.

As a single man for the last 4 years, great sexual encounters with women have been a rare luxury. My iPhone, on the other hand, is all too willing to dance for me, undress for me, tease me, lick me, suck me, screw me and all around indulge me, whatever I want, any time I want.

I do not generally have an addictive personality, yet I have at times gone weeks using internet pornography every night to quickly arouse and then satiate myself. There were times I seemed to need it just to fall asleep. I would watch up to an hour or more in bed before exhausting myself enough to fall asleep, which ironically carved into an already sleep-deprived entrepreneurial lifestyle. At one point using porn actually gave me repetitive stress injury, messing up my otherwise formidable basketball game. I experienced other disconcerting side-effects of porn, too, some of which I'll detail below.

There's nothing wrong with masturbation. I also don't believe in sexual shame. But modern pornography can be a serious detriment to everyone, not just to men, but to the women we love, too.

Here's 6 reasons why I believe men must give up consistent use of pornography for personal stimulation:

1. Porn ruins our erections with actual women.
(ref: http://globalnews.ca/news/1232726/porn-causing-erectiledysfunction-in-young-men/)

After I had been using porn moderately for about a year, I began to notice that I couldn't sustain erections with women as long as I once could. I was horny as ever, but without the constantly changing visual erotic stimulation that watching video after video offered, one woman's body couldn't hold my erotic focus as effectively as it used to. To my frustrated surprise, real sex had become somewhat under-stimulating. Tragic. Since I gave up porn, even morning wood has made its return like an exotic tree rescued from the brink of extinction.

2. Porn tunes our bodies to premature ejaculation.
(ref: http://www.psychologytoday.com/blog/all-about-sex/201005/premature-ejaculation-the-two-causes-mens-1-sex-problem)

I never had a problem with quick climax before I consistently used porn. I could always match, if not outlast, my female sexual partners, with or without a condom and always with solid erections.

With porn, I could watch a short video and within minutes have myself rocketing towards climax. But I'd stop myself before I went too far, because I always wanted to see what different erotic adventure awaited me in the next video, just a click away. I would do this for an hour, rapidly rising in mindless bliss with every new short video, stopping myself at the edge each time. Eventually, I'd realize how much time had gone by, so I'd choose the best video I'd seen and let it throw me over the edge.

I was tuning my body to quickly rise and climax. I can immediately stop moving my own hand when I masturbate. A real woman's aroused body doesn't stop moving so fast. It's like trying to slam on the brakes of a speed boat in deep water. I just couldn't often handle her enthusiasm, and I started getting really concerned.

Thankfully, quitting porn has allowed my body's nervous system to retune itself to a less hurried sexual pace and rhythm.

3. It's a cop out from interacting powerfully with actual women.

Most men in our western culture generally do not know how to interact powerfully with women in the everyday world, certainly not as mature healthy masculine men. We routinely fail to proactively step up to women we're attracted to in effective and honorable, respectful ways. So many of us routinely let our silent crushes slip away forever into the dark painful cave of our regrets. Masturbation can take the edge off all the resulting frustration, so much so that we don't then have to do anything useful about it, like learn how to be more powerful (and still respectful) in our interactions with actual women.

4. It's a colossal waste of precious time.

Watch porn alone isn't what you came to this planet to do. Get on with your deepest purpose, already, or with finding out what that is if you don't yet know.

5. It creates unrealistic expectations of women.

Porn just makes men think women should be easier to get into bed. It makes us think we might get laid more if we were more bold or clever, or simply more aggressive. Which is actually probably true. In fact, there is surely room for western men to be bolder with women, but not at the cost of genuine care for women.

Women in porn videos are always willing to let a man (or men) aggressively open them up and do whatever they want. They'll take the money shot right in the face, on their knees beneath a cock and a camera, as if to fully underscore their willingness to be conquered and owned by a man, and for all the world to see.

In my experience, actual women don't react to calculating male aggression by opening their legs. Even if they do – and sometimes they probably do – that doesn't create an authentic intimate relationship. It just creates two bodies slapping into each other.

Women are lusty, sexual creatures, for sure. Just like men. But when men are ready to relate to women in deeper ways, ways that include sexuality and also transcend it, porn is an awful study. The wondrous feminine mystique of a woman, the mystique us men so desperately crave to experience, is only made available to the men who learn how to cherish a woman in her fullness. That doesn't happen anywhere in porn.

6. When we watch porn, we support human trafficking, slavery, rape, and blackmail of women all over the world.
(ref: http://www.wnd.com/2013/11/porns-part-in-sex-trafficking/)

Despite my tame taste in porn and the fact that I never paid for online porn, I still unwittingly saw videos on the average free porn site that disturbed me. I am horrified that I almost surely watched men manipulate, even outright blackmail, women into otherwise unwanted sex in fake taxi cabs, fake doctors offices, fake casting sets, and more. The camera rarely showed the man's face; always the woman's.

Since I started researching this, I've discovered countless examples of criminal cases worldwide where people, mostly men, have been arrested and prosecuted for creating pornography with women they trafficked from other countries; women who were enslaved in buildings they couldn't leave; women kept in place by physical violence; women threatened with exposure to their families; and more. I know now that I must have watched videos where women did sex acts they were forced to do. And my tastes in porn were tame.

I'm not implying there's definitely a direct link between porn and criminality. Surely a lot of porn is filmed with consenting female adults. I am simply saying I couldn't easily avoid watching videos of questionable, disturbing origin, and that this is not an overall good thing for humanity.

I'm still tempted to watch porn sometimes. Even as I write this, my iPhone sits quietly beside me, able in a matter of seconds to unleash a marauding army of sexy oriental babysitters straight into my lizard brain. But clearly nothing good ever comes from that, so to speak.

Men, we've got to stop using porn. I know it's a quick fix. I know some couples even use it to spice up an otherwise fading sex life. I say find other ways. Get creative.

Porn is easy, low-hanging fruit, beneath our brilliance. It's not just hurting us; it's also hurting our women.

 *7*

6 THINGS AN EVOLVED MAN WANTS FROM A WOMAN

I hear women often talk about wanting an evolved, conscious man. I've decided that mostly means they want to be with a man who can see a woman's entire humanity, the profound gifts she has to offer as a feminine woman and a human being, before focusing on her ass. He has also embraced his own internal dose of femininity, so he can truly embrace the feminine women in his midst. There's surely more to say about that, but I don't want to make a big production of this point. I won't claim to actually be an evolved man, anyway, which might disqualify me if I did. I still eat cheeseburgers, so.

Nonetheless, a brilliant mature woman I consider to be evolved recently asked me what an evolved man wants from a woman. So with her inquiry as my sole credential, here goes:

1. He wants her full authentic self.

An evolved man wants a woman who won't change to be with him, who mostly doesn't give two sheets what other people think about her, including even him. She isn't arrogant; she just knows who she is and doesn't need to prove that she has the right to live however she desires. Sure, they might have to make difficult choices in the details of their life together (aka "compromise"), but she doesn't shrink or sell herself out to make him happy. It won't.

He won't criticize her for being her authentic self, either.

An evolved man longs to see his woman radiant and genuinely happy. If she isn't thrilled about her everyday life, he won't be, either. Not because she's responsible for his feelings (she's not), but because the second best gift she could ever give him is her own authentic happiness, which brings me to #2 …

2. He wants her authentic happiness.

An evolved man has no sinister desire to capture a woman's joyful heart in an iron box and isolate her in a household castle. No. He just wants his woman so in love with her life that her radiant joy is present in the room more often than not. Yes there will be tough times. He won't expect her to always be happy; he doesn't want some spooky Stepford Wife with a fake smile. He simply wants her aware enough to know that she's responsible for her own happiness.

He'll be doing his best to be a good man for her, but he doesn't want to be burdened with "making her happy."

He's busy enough trying to manage his own experience. Understanding this allows both partners to safely bring their real truths to the relationship every day, which is essential to sustaining real intimacy … which is what an evolved man truly wants.

3. He wants her to love him with wild abandon.

Many years ago I witnessed a new bride gaze with such absolute adoration upon her new husband's face that I felt the Earth jealous even though it had the Sun. An evolved man wants his woman to radiate her love all over him like that. He will do his best to earn that from her, but then again … what has the Earth ever done to earn the Sun?

An evolved man wants his woman to love him profoundly despite his imperfections, to consistently see through his human flaws to the very best of him.

There's an important caveat, however, as so many women are great at loving with wild abandon, but in a way that's often self-defeating. An evolved man doesn't want a woman to abandon herself to love him or stay if he consistently acts horribly, failing to honor their agreements (an evolved man can still fall victim to messing up big time; he's human, after all). Which brings me urgently to #4 ...

4. He wants her to communicate openly and even call out his bullshit ... but respectfully.

An evolved man wants a woman who will speak her truth to him, a woman who knows men aren't equipped to read minds or even not-so-subtle clues.

He also wants her to hold him accountable to his highest potential as a man, and always with love and respect.

He does not want her looking for every flaw in an attempt to make him perfect. That's just annoying. But he also doesn't want her to hold back when she sees him acting out of integrity or playing small in his life. An intimate relationship is a powerful vehicle for a person's evolution, and he knows he'll always be growing and evolving. He wants a woman who will support him in that evolution, and who's also learned the difference between healthy, honest communication and needling criticism.

5. He wants her to surrender ... to Love.

When I originally wrote this article in 2014, my ideas on "surrender" were a bit "less evolved."

At the time, I essentially wrote this: "An evolved man doesn't even try to possess a woman. He doesn't want her to abandon her dreams or live only for him. He wants her to live fully in her truth. However, he does want her to relax and trust him primarily to lead their lives together. An evolved man doesn't want 50/50 decision-making in his intimate relationship. When two people dance together, only one can lead."

I understand now that the true power in surrender is never in surrendering your will to another person's will.

The real power in surrender is in surrendering your will to LOVE.

An unconscious relationship is a battle of egos living together mostly in fear. When both partners are living in their own ego stories (L.I.E.S. = Living In Ego Stories), it means they are believing fear-based thoughts that create anxiety and stress. For example:

> *"My partner must act a certain way to prove he/she loves me."*
> *"My partner needs to change to make me happy."*
> *"My partner needs to trust my decision making."*
> *"I'm afraid my partner will lie to me, so I need to keep a close eye on his/her behavior."*

… and so on.

A relationship in which fear-based thinking dominates the dynamic will inevitably create an exhausting power struggle. Things will either stagnate in a stalemate or outright suck.

What does it mean to surrender to Love?

Surrendering to Love means being willing to do your own inner work to recognize when your choices, actions, words are emerging out of fear (aka your survival-concerned ego), and learning how to shift yourself towards living from a mindset of love. In other words, it means learning to trust in love over fear.

(Note: There's far more to this than I'll explore here. I support people in doing this fear-to-love inner work in my coaching practice, and I've been doing this essential work with my own coaches for years.)

An evolved man is only "evolved" in that he's learning to trust in love over his ego's fears. Naturally, he wants his woman evolving in the same direction. If she's not actively learning to trust in love, herself, then she's going to remain stuck believing in her own ego's fears.

When you trust in your fears, there's no room for authentic love. When fear clouds the space between two people, you can't see each other clearly. You can only see projections of your fear. To be clear, trusting in love doesn't mean tolerating abusive or violating behavior. Quite the opposite, trusting in love means trusting that love will show the way forward in every moment in ways that ultimately yield the highest good for all. Sometimes surrendering to love means allowing the relationship to end.

The reason trusting in love is difficult for most of us – and why there are surely so few "evolved men" (or women) on the planet – is because it means your ego won't always (or even often) get its way. Yet this is the only way a relationship can be truly, deeply, sustainably fulfilling.

A relationship with a woman who trusts her fear and ego more than love is a relationship that will likely devolve into the pitiable cliche in which she has his metaphorical balls in a metaphorical jar. Her fear controls their lives because they've created a pattern in which he needs her permission for every decision.

Eventually, she won't want to fuck him anymore, because she's attracted to a man with balls. A man with balls is fully committed to his highest purpose, which is Love, not her ego (or his). It's a sad irony.

A woman who wants to strap his balls to her vagina won't do well with an evolved man.

He doesn't need or even want her permission to live his purpose everyday, whatever that looks like for him. His woman's ego and fear cannot ever be his purpose. Because Love is his highest purpose, it will be excruciating to him to be with a woman who is not surrendered to Love as hers, too.

6. He wants her surrendered sexually, too.

Culturally, we've created immense amounts of shame around sexuality. It's time we set that insanity on fire, with our loins.

An evolved man will definitely continue wanting sex. Passionate. Consistent. Unbridled. Anytime. Sex. He'll want no petty psychological or emotional games around sex from his partner (role-playing and other such games excepted) – no intentional withholding and no tit-for-that negotiating.

An evolved man would rather negotiate with terrorists than negotiate for sex with his intimate partner.

To be clear: An evolved man will never take his woman sexually when she doesn't want him to, whether she says no with actual words or non-verbally with her body. That's called rape even if you're married, and it's always wrong.

But as he will want a woman surrendered to Love, that means she will be surrendered to her deeply-felt sexual nature, too.

Because she is surrendered to Love, she will be deeply connected to her inner radiant, sensual feminine essence which she can then enthusiastically, wholeheartedly, and with sincere pleasure offer to him. Sexuality will be a natural extension of her self-love practice and she'll therefore likely enjoy sex as much as he does (and probably more).

He accepts that she won't always be willing or even able – when she's in physical or emotional pain, for example – and he won't ever make her guilty for it. Which may turn her on even more.

He is also surrendered to Love, so he will always be deeply sensitive to her needs. Still, he won't castrate himself internally to protect her from his sexuality. Such internal castration – so common in today's men – diminishes a man's power in the presence of a woman, which I believe then causes men to rely on porn, strip clubs, massage parlors, shallow affairs, etc. as substitutes for the real thing.

A woman not consistently surrendered to love in her own being, which just means a woman loyal only to her own ego and fears, inevitably becomes a woman sexually shut off from him.

When his woman is consistently shut off to him sexually, there's clearly a disconnect between them – a disconnect from Love – and he'll want to explore that together. It could be the way he's showing up in their relationship. It could be bio-chemical. It could be something else. But he'll want to explore it. He'll want her to want to explore it openly with him, too.

That's what evolved couples do: Communicate deeply, vulnerably, with appreciation for differences, with the ultimate goal of creating pure fucking magic together, every single day.

One last thing on #6: an evolved man won't make his ejaculation (or hers for that matter) the purpose of sex. But that's a whole other essay.

In the end, an evolved man doesn't actually want anything in particular from a woman other than her authentic self. He's self-satisfied, so she's free to be whoever she wants to be.

He'll certainly recognize when things are off and want to explore that with her. But he won't make her responsible for his happiness, either, and he won't ever ask her to live inauthentically for him. If ever he does, he'll be aware enough to see that his request just points to some personal internal confusion he hasn't quite reconciled with yet.

She's still off the hook for his happiness.

8

THE MASCULINE SEARCH FOR FREEDOM (WHY IT MATTERS TO YOU)

Ignorance of the masculine and feminine energies at play in our intimate relationships – straight or otherwise – can wreak utter havoc.

Many years ago, my life changed dramatically when author David Deida taught me that the masculine nature in any man (or woman) is always seeking freedom.

The "masculine" I learned is that primal force in us all that compels us to push beyond any limitation imposed on us by the world around us – and within us. It's that onward urge that makes us create airplanes and rockets to break the heavy bonds of gravity so we can travel freely throughout the heavens.

The world's economic system is set up such that the more money we make, the more social freedom we have to go wherever and do whatever we want. Thus the widespread obsession with making money. No one wants stacks of thin green paper piled high around in their living room; we want the social freedom it provides in the system mostly masculine people have created.

Political leaders – like terrorists – always know how to rile up their base with cries of freedom: *"Give me freedom or give me death!"* (even if that means denying freedom to others).

Consider sports. They're only about creating constraints (sidelined fields, dimensioned courts, groomed fairways, etc.), putting a worthy adversary in front of us (a team, one person, ourselves), and pushing at our limits until we break through to that one place that lives just beyond both adversary and constraint: the basket, goal, hole, end zone, finish line. If you've ever felt high after kicking a ball into a goal while 11 people tried to stop you, or you just watched your favorite team do so, you know the ecstatic thrill of embodied freedom through sport.

The "feminine" I also learned isn't so concerned with the search for freedom. She never screams, *"Set me free!"* Actually, she aches for the opposite.

[Note: Although I use "she" as the feminine and "he" as the masculine, all men and women have both masculine and feminine energy. It's not a genital, gender or sex thing.]

Feminine energy carries our longing for the embodied experience of love, radiance and beauty. She's always saying in endless ways, *"Show me the love!"*

Deida wrote that the essential masculine plea is, *"I want out of here!"* That doesn't mean a man (or masculine-identified woman) always wants to run away, but rather that his masculine nature is going to have him constantly seeking ways to escape the constraints he experiences in the world around and within him. Which sometimes means staying put and fighting through difficulties or constraints.

Stand-up comic, Patrice O'Neal, in a bit he does which you can see online, makes the face of a man in love: a scrunched-up dissatisfied look of exhausted resignation. Then he makes the face of a woman in love: happy and carefree. *"Yay!"* he exclaims while acting out a woman's face in love. The audience laughs, of course, because reality is entertaining. The cliche of relationship as trapped man with eager woman looms large in our collective consciousness.

Again, I want to be clear this isn't actually a "man v. woman" thing. Both men and woman express masculine and feminine energy. However, like author Marianne Williamson says, most people in their lives are majoring in either masculinity or femininity and minoring in the other. While it is typically men who major in masculinity, some women are majoring in it, too, just as some men major in femininity.

Here's the point:

Awareness of the archetypal forces at play in our intimate relationships can make it easier to see why they are often so challenging.

Our ignorance sabotages us. Our high divorce rates aren't falling, and might even be rising. Awareness can help us move through our challenges with more grace.

But no one ever teaches us the differences between femininity and masculinity. Worse, we're taught to prefer shallow expressions of masculine energy and deny, dismiss or only exploit all expressions of feminine.

Which is partly why my parents – and probably yours – clearly only knew how to just "wing it" through multiple strained marriages. No one ever taught them any better, either.

Many years ago, I lived with a girlfriend who was far more feminine in her essence than I. She loved to bring in little crystals and seashells from the beach to make our home pretty. She loved to wear glitter and sparkly jewelry and hear from me how beautiful I thought she was. She had an office job, and she was brilliant at it, but her passion was children. Her biggest dream was building a home on a small plot of land in Argentina that her parents owned, having a garden with a fish pond and raising a family with me. Deeply connected to the femininity flowing through her, she was never really concerned about freedom from anything, except perhaps having to work.

She was only always obsessed with whether or not I really loved her.

The basic pattern of our downward doom spiral was this:

Uncertainty caused her to demand evidence of my love that made sense to her. I resented her attempts to constrain my behavior (i.e. change me in ways that she felt would prove I loved her). This made her feel more uncertain and make even more desperate demands. Which I further resisted and resented.

Wash, rinse and repeat for 5 years, until there's no joy left, and whatever love you once had is now buried under a putrid mountain of resentment, anger and pain.

We thought we were fighting about jealousy, or who was sacrificing more, or who hurt who first. But we were never fighting about those things. We were only always fighting about her deepest desire to actually feel love between us, and about my deepest desire to actually feel my freedom.

Had I been aware that the feminine force in her was yearning to experience the depths of my love, I could have shown up completely differently for her. Had she understood that the masculine force in me was only yearning for freedom to live on my own terms, she could have been more thoughtful about not forcing me into actions she thought would comfort her.

Of course she had a masculine desire for freedom, too. She didn't want me telling her what to do, either. Just as I had a feminine desire to feel her love and not be abandoned by her. But she mostly got angry when she saw me do things that suggested I didn't love her enough. I mostly got angry when I felt she would never let me be who I freely wanted to be.

In any intimate relationship, whether between a man and a woman or two women or two men, where that tingly electricity flows that we all so deeply crave, the archetypical energies of masculine and feminine are at play. Like the opposite poles of a powerful magnet, these forces can draw us inexorably, mysteriously, irresistibly, ecstatically towards each other. But if we don't recognize the different melodies and rhythms inherent in each of their unique expressions, we will only experience a mad cacophony in their clashing that will eventually exhaust us and have us begging for silence.

Men are not defective versions of women. Women are not defective versions of men. There are primal archetypical energies at play in all of us, which iconic psychiatrist Carl Jung began mapping out 100 years ago.

I was ignorant of those different rhythms for 25 years, and that ignorance cost me every good woman I ever tried to love.

A PRACTICE

If you're more core Feminine: Look for how your more masculine partner's actions and complaints may point to their general search for freedom. Notice this and see if you can enthusiastically support their desire for freedom in creative ways that are still in alignment with your desires.

If you're more core Masculine: Notice whether your partner's actions or complaints may point to uncertainty around your commitment to the relationship, or to them. They might simply not feel the full presence of your love. You might not actually be giving it if – particularly if you're working too much, watching a lot of TV, using porn, or just don't know how to listen well. Try to see beneath their complaint and demonstrate your love in ways they will understand. They'll be more at ease once they feel the full depth of your masculine presence and love. You might even find this makes resolving their complaints a lot easier!

There are surely a lot of subtleties to this exploration, as we all express both masculine and feminine energies. But this is a good place to start. Even a little awareness of these masculine-feminine dynamics can make a huge difference in your intimate experiences.

9

HOW TO
COMPLIMENT A WOMAN

There's only one right way to compliment a woman: Freely, with no expectation that she'll give us anything in return for it.

There's only one place a genuine compliment arises from: Genuine appreciation of whatever gift she's giving to the world in this moment.

Whether that gift be her radiant femininity, her intelligence, her presence, her physical beauty, her smile, her cleverness, her strength, her love. Whatever she is offering the world in this moment, a compliment is well-suited to tell a woman that her presence is genuinely cherished.

When a man can offer a woman such an acknowledgment, freely and sincerely with no expectation of anything in return from her, everyone feels great. Acknowledging and appreciating beauty in the world is a pleasure, in and of itself.

Unfortunately, too many men only compliment women when they want something from her: a smile, acknowledgment, validation, a phone number, sex, feminine energy, whatever, anything.

A viral video recently made the rounds, showing a woman walking through the streets of New York, approached, followed, harassed, catcalled, propositioned, objectified more than 10 times every hour. That video is only ugly because we immediately get that all those men want something from her that she doesn't want to offer, and they don't care that she feels uncomfortable by their presence. Their selfish, narcissistic disregard for her well-being is viscerally offensive to the sensitive heart.

Men, can you imagine being constantly approached by total strangers who want something from you, who are physically stronger than you and would almost surely take what they want if they thought they could get away with it?

It isn't just city-street men who make women feel uncomfortable in public.

I was in Starbucks recently when I saw a well-to-do 50-something-year-old man and a Starbucks employee start impishly elbowing each other when an attractive woman walked in the store in that way adolescent boys do. I felt nauseous, myself, just watching these two grown men mentally gang-bang her as she waited to order a latté (I'm guessing).

We have no idea how powerful we truly are, or where our authentic power resides. We tend to think our power is in our sheer force of will. Our persistence. Our insistence. Our cleverness. Our anger. Our testicles.

Yes, there's power in those places. We use them constantly to persist, coerce, manipulate, shame, berate, and cajole women into giving us what we want. Then we wonder why so many women have a hard time trusting most men.

But that's not where we're most powerful.

A man's true power is in his heart.

When a man can only hold the world and women as objects in his endlessly strategizing mind, he will use both only as tools to serve his little ego self. Such a man will use the limited battery power contained in his will, persistence or cleverness, in his anger or in his testicles, to get whatever he wants from the world and from women. Even if he has to manipulate, exploit, coerce, or oppress. Such a man will tend to create a lot of collateral damage as he constantly maneuvers to sustain his flickering power.

However, a man connected to his heart is a man who radiates power like the sun.

He will hold both the world and women with appreciation and respect for their beauty, their life-giving force, their innate mysterious wisdom and infinite gift of love energy. Such a man will treat a woman completely differently: he won't expect her to return his gift of appreciation and cherishing, though he'll certainly welcome it when she offers it freely. He'll experience an authentic power beyond measure.

That may be poetic, but consider that a feminine woman actually wants her beauty appreciated by men. She enhances her physical appearance with jewelry, make-up, perfume, and attractive clothing so that she will be noticed and appreciated.

A man in his heart will absolutely appreciate a woman's beauty, and he can express that appreciation in all kinds of ways that won't make her feel uncomfortable.

He can even enjoy in her presence the sexual charge that rises in his body like that electric tingle in summer air before a thunderstorm—without making her feel like she has to do something about it. She may not want to do anything about it for him, and he'll be ok with that because he holds her in his heart. Concern for her well-being is primary in his heart. And she'll feel that. She'll instinctively trust him because of it. A new world is born.

Because she trusts him, a woman may open to a man even more in the presence of a genuine compliment, like a beautiful flower opening to the sun, eager to offer its hidden gift to the world. She loves being deeply appreciated, cherished, and a genuine compliment communicates this to her. This is the power of real love. Only a man in his heart can access such power.

Still, a man in his heart doesn't ask anything in return for his compliments, not even acknowledgment.

For he knows she might not give it, but only because we have a lot of collective work to do earn women's collective trust back. And we men do have a lot of collective work to do to earn back women's trust.

Women have been mishandled daily for ages, in the streets, at the office, in their homes, by their friends and acquaintances and strangers, by too many men disconnected from their hearts and so challenged to see beyond merely the advantages a woman can offer them. We men can be thoughtful about that.

We can still give women compliments, too, which most surely welcome so long as we don't demand anything in return. When we offer a genuine compliment to a woman, we simply offer a gift:

Our pure appreciation.

As we likewise feel great and fulfilled in the giving of our appreciation, with no expectation for anything in return, not even a "thank you," everyone wins.

 **10**

WHAT A WOMAN REALLY WANTS ISN'T A MAN'S MONEY

Twice in my life, I have made a lot of money only to adventure it all away.

At 26, I had built up substantial savings as a young US Air Force Officer. I had a sweet pad by the Atlantic Ocean, a Sebring convertible and the means to properly entertain my Canadian girlfriend whenever and however I wanted.

But as I slipped deeper into a secret depression, I left the military desperate to save my own life. Like Brad Pitt's character in the movie, "Legends of The Fall," with a far-away stare and an empty heart, I one day up and flew off into the world, breaking my girlfriend's precious heart – mine had already long been broken. I spent the next three years chasing dark shadows and seductive sirens, throwing myself into one brief and tormented love affair after the next, until finally, at age 29, I was kicked out of France by a soon-to-be ex-wife.

During that particular misadventure, I gave my French wife money, took her on trips, paid the rent, and bought her jewelry and cigarettes. Still, she booted me out less than a year after we started, fed up with the man she married. When I landed hard back in the USA, all I had left was a freshly broken heart, a few stories you wouldn't believe, a few bucks in my bank account and no obvious future.

I went to heal in Miami at my dad's place. I spent the next few years helping him grow a $50 million business from zero, accumulating another small fortune for myself. With newly deep pockets, I moved in with a beautiful woman from South America. I was able to offer her most anything money could buy. We had a nice home, a cat, money to travel and play with. We had all the makings of a good life.

Unfortunately, my bank account refused to fund our happiness. If anything, it just poured miracle grow on our dysfunction.

At 34, I walked away from that company and its big paychecks. I left that passionate Latin woman, too, to tour and manage an independent music band. I had money and time, so I worked purely for the love of an otherworldly music that had infected me.

A few years and countless adventures later, I was 38, living in Los Angeles, and near broke. The band had split up and I had once again spent all my scratch. I was couch surfing through friends' homes, hustling for work with Los Angeles' vast world of artists and dreamers for often little or no money.

I was single and starting over for the third time.

A few years later, I was a published author, a well-read blogger and an impassioned life & relationship coach to men and women, still working to create a new fortune to provide for myself and a good woman.

I still didn't have that fortune. Or that woman. But I did have an invaluable lesson carved from the failures of my relationships passed:

A modern woman doesn't need me for my money or my resources. What she needs is my full, embodied masculine presence. She needs to know I'm actually here, that I see and feel her deeply, and that I'm not going anywhere.

Women don't need men like they used to. We're living through a pivotal moment in history when women are achieving social and economic equality with men. They no longer need us for access to resources – security, money, sustenance, social influence, etc.

Which is great! For humanity to thrive, women must have equal influence and access throughout society.

Still, it's a disorienting time for many of us, particularly in intimate relationships. There remains an inordinate amount of social pressure on men to be capable of providing tangible resources in exchange for a woman's company. The ability to make things happen in the world is easily measured by dollars and cars and houses and things, which in turn remains presumed evidence of a man's masculine prowess and vitality.

But none of that is a measure of his heart.

Most any modern woman – even one who energizes a lot of masculine energy in her life – yearns to know her partner cherishes her and will always show up for her. She wants to know he won't check out and leave, which many men do even when we stay in the room.

Can he remain present when the relationship is strained? When she acts irrational and difficult, unknowingly presenting herself as an apparent problem he cannot solve, can he love her fully, anyway? This is the true measure of a man's heart.

A woman with a strong internal feminine essence aches to relax into her masculine partner's strength and care. She wants to know she can trust him, that he genuinely cherishes her and will step up and do what must be done to ensure the safety of her world.

That's why access to resources has long been a measure of a man's worthiness, and why it's an outdated measure.

As a relationship coach to both men and women, I see over and over that when a man is able to show up and be fully present – heart, mind, and body – with his partner, she is instinctively able to relax. She will then follow that man most anywhere, even if she has to ride the bus with him to get there. If he can't show up for her (or doesn't know how), even if that man has all the money in the world, she'll eventually ache for a man who can. She'll either try to pull it out of the man she's with, or she'll switch off her heart (and body), and look for that masculine presence elsewhere, possibly in her children, or at work, in another friendship, or in her own being.

That's what I was doing when I was young, moneyed, and ignorant. I thought my partners would be happy there was money and entertainment. I got confused and resentful when they weren't satisfied with the world I thought they wanted. I didn't get that what they really wanted was to feel the full commitment of my love far more than mere access to my wallet and a nice home.

Sure, a nice home and money to pay the bills is important in the modern world, but so many of us men still focus primarily on pursuing material resources to make ourselves worthy of a woman's love. In doing so, we overlook her deeper yearning. Even many women aren't aware of this yearning in their hearts.

A few years ago, I pursued a woman when my resources were stressed. I knew I couldn't then provide things for her that other men could. She was a woman of means, anyway; she didn't need mine. I decided instead that I could give her the gift of my incessantly curious mind, my laughter and playfulness, my relentless optimism, my kindness and my listening.

I knew I could show her that she is completely safe in my presence, and that I was a man who could fully cherish her heart. By the endlessly beaming smile on her face in my presence, I knew I was onto something.

I can offer all that to any woman, anytime, no matter my cash flow. My painful past has proven that loving presence is far more valuable, anyway.

Any man can offer his loving presence to his partner. His money might affect where he lives or vacations, but it can never define his worth as a Man. It also can't buy him harmony in an intimate relationship.

I will create another fortune, though I can't know how long it will take. In the meantime, I just keep fully showing up for the woman I'm choosing, and who is also choosing me. Sometimes in life, fully showing up is all I can offer. Fortunately, it's what most modern women these days are deeply aching for in love.

11

HOW TO GET ANYONE TO FALL IN LOVE WITH YOU

When I was in college, a male friend and I were surveying a group of attractive young women at a party when he leaned towards me and quietly whispered with an unforgettable air of smug confidence, *"Bryan, don't you feel sometimes like you could make any woman in the world fall in love with you?"*

I didn't know what he was talking about.

I dismissed his question as arrogant and deluded.

I didn't have it easy with women. I believed women were downright difficult to convince. Besides, I couldn't see in me whatever they might see in me. Getting a woman to fall in love with me was always going to be hard, so I thought. I now believe he was striking at a truth underneath all that youthful arrogance.

Naturally, we humans are all ever-eager to fall deeply, passionately, exquisitely in love with one another. The experience of authentic love is simply awesome. It's mostly our protective facades and fears – and perhaps a little chemistry – that ever prevent love from happening effortlessly.

As I've matured and come to more deeply know myself and appreciate the innate beauty within my own being, I've learned that creating the opportunity for love to blossom with another person is rather easy. It merely requires the following elements:

1. Authenticity & Vulnerability

True intimacy is only possible through vulnerability, which means being honest about who I am. Nobody likes to be manipulated, and that's what our social masks are designed to do: manipulate other people's opinions and behavior in our favor. But a sensitive, open heart can feel through the facade, and one's carefully prepared fictions don't interest an open heart. We yearn to feel the truth in one another. The Real. We ache for the Real.

Authenticity and vulnerability can be wildly sexy because they are acts of openly offering ourselves as Real as we come. Besides, when you see me honor and share my Real you feel more comfortable to honor and share yours. Which brings me to …

2. Radical Acceptance

Each of us ultimately wants to be accepted for who we really are. It's exhausting trying to be someone else. When I am able to communicate to a woman that I can truly hold all of her, from her radiance to her pain, she can't help but start to love me for that. Of course, to be able to fully accept a woman from her radiance to her pain requires that a man connect to the true source of his power: his heart.

3. Connection to Heart

A man's true power isn't in his brains or his balls. It's in his heart. He can't fully accept a woman and her vast and complex range of emotional expression if he lives from brain or balls alone. His logical brain only works to solve the apparently endless problems she seems to pose for him, and his balls merely want her to gratify his needs.

It's only the deep love radiating from his own illogical heart that can continue loving her when she inevitably shows up looking like a problem his logical brain can't solve, or she won't satisfy his lusty balls. Only a man connected to his heart can cherish a woman in her wild and radiant fullness.

In a world that often tells her she's either too much or not enough, most any woman is aching for a heart-connected partner who can fully cherish her however she shows up in this unpredictable moment.

4. Confident Sexuality

Oh, the sexual shame and disorientation that still runs rampant through our modern world. For much of my life, I wasn't always clear what to do with the sexual passions that would rage through my body like wildfire. The world mostly taught me to hide them lest I be discovered for the perverted creature I apparently wasn't supposed to be.

So I often hid these passions from women, worried they would be frightened by me – at least until their tongues in my mouth gave me reason to suspect otherwise. As a result, I let countless available women slip quietly away who might otherwise have fallen in love with me had I shown them in healthy, heart-connected ways that I was, in fact, cherishingly starving for them and not content on loitering long in the friend-zone.

It took me a while, and admittedly, a healthy amount of sex with ravenous women, to realize that women are just as genuinely jazzed about sex as I am.

Sexuality is a wondrous gift. It is nothing to be ashamed of. Wielding it responsibly, ethically and in ways connected to heart, is an art form. But when embraced and perfected, this art form can inspire the most intimate parts of our being to arch backwards in eye-popping ecstasy and dissolve us blissfully into love, even before actual physical intercourse happens.

5. Patience

Nothing inspires a woman's love more than a man in whose presence she can relax, knowing he won't push her to do what she doesn't yet want to do.

Nothing says, *"I am a safe, strong place for you to relax your weary self,"* more than showing a woman I have no intention to push her to do something before she's ready to. And nothing inspires a woman's love more than a man in whose presence she can relax her weary self, knowing he won't push her to do what she doesn't yet want to do.

That essentially means being clear with her about what I want from her – whether her time, affection, sex, or whatever – while assuring her that I'm already enough in love with my own life that I don't need anything from her to be happy already. I'm self-contained and self-satisfied. Into my pre-satisfied patience, then, she gets the great joy of offering her authentic gifts: her radiance, her brilliance, her smile, her love.

That's all most anyone really wants to do in life: give their authentic gifts to the world, and to each other.

One could argue that other factors are essential too, like chemistry and timing. However, could it be that we are all powerful chemists capable of creating love reactions simply by mixing in the right empowering ingredients? Perhaps.

Regardless, I was blind to how ever present is the opportunity for love to blossom until I started seeing just how much we all deeply yearn to fall in love with each other.

Now, as I turn 40 and reflect back on my entire life of relationships with women, I'm learning just how powerful I am – have always been even though I didn't know it – to create the space within which a woman can fall in love with me, and I with her, simply by showing up in my own raw authenticity, connected to heart, passionately connected to my truth and actively fascinated to explore hers.

Throw in patience and a sprinkle of time and voila! a recipe for creating the experience of falling in love, regardless whether or not we follow through with it.

 12

5 SIGNS A MAN IS CONNECTED TO HIS HEART

"The wound is the place where the light enters you."
– Rumi

Many men think our power is in our brains or our balls. Our rational brains are supposed to do all the figuring out while our testosterone-filled balls supply the driving force.

Intelligence. Determination. Courage. Sheer force of will. These are the masculine convictions of our brains and our balls. And they're absolutely valid and essential in their own way. But when used in isolation from our true power source for too long, they leave us dead inside, unable to deeply connect with life – including our intimate partners.

When I was a US military officer, I was trained to use those masculine brains-n-balls convictions to accomplish whatever the mission, whatever the cost. After 10 years of operating purely on brains and balls alone, I was completely dead inside. I couldn't really laugh. I couldn't at all cry. I had an amazing girlfriend I couldn't really love. I couldn't feel much of anything.

I didn't realize then that the military takes to the extreme what modern culture idolizes: the prioritization of rationality over emotion; the worship of intellectual understanding over embodied knowing. The military intentionally disconnects the brains and balls from embodied knowing because that's our direct connection to the actual, tangible, visceral life we're immersed in every moment, regardless what our brains have to say about it.

The military knows that you can't take life when you feel connected to life.

Men, particularly, routinely deny this powerful embodied connection to life that we cannot experience through our thinking brains alone. Yet this power center is what enables us to deeply feel our own lives, to feel the world, and to then create truly extraordinary relationships with other people and lives in which we thrive everyday.

Truly, when we live from this innate power source which connects us to life, itself, we can make entire worlds thrive. This power source isn't in our brains or our balls. It's in the heart.

We men tend to think of "heart" as merely something to help us win the close game or appeal to a woman's romantic side. That's like thinking the sun is only good for frying ants.

A man genuinely connected to his heart, who lives each day with his brain and balls in proper service to his heart's deeper wisdom, is a man that breathes life into the world. He can inspire and lift up the world, even if it's only one person's world.

How does a man connected to heart show up everyday, not just when his team is down 5 points with a minute remaining? What does such a man look like?

1. He's deeply patient.

With himself. With others. With life.

When we're connected to heart, we're able to be patient with and authentically love life, ourselves and other people, even when they don't do what we want them to do – which is almost always.

In the military, I was so disconnected from my heart that I hated life. I was imprisoned in my brain. Sex was my only escape. The day I left base for the last time, I headed for the open road with only a backpack and pent-up rage. Little did I know, I was also heading into the darkest night my soul has ever experienced.

That dark night waxed and waned for 12 years and involved angry women and drugs and heartbreak and financial ruin. I was always impatient for the rest of the world to change so I could finally feel good, and I acted out in countless ways to make it change. By its end, my ego had been gutted so profoundly, as I finally had to accept just how little I am in control of anything or anyone and just how messy life is no matter what I do to keep it clean. With every smash against the rocks I took, every despairing night and furious girlfriend, the heavy armor surrounding my heart cracked and weakened until I gradually discovered an abiding peace and a laughter I had never felt in my body before.

When I finally emerged from that dark night, I found myself in a new reality that showed me we are all innocent in our ignorance. We are each doing the best we can, all the time, even when it doesn't look that way. If we truly knew how to do things better, we'd do it.

That one insight gave me access to an embodied patience with people, myself, with life, that I had never known, that no one ever taught me. That insight was borne of a freshly opened heart.

Granted, my patience remains a work in progress for my brain and my balls still constantly seek to assert their authority. But my heart is no longer slave to my brain or my balls. I can move powerfully towards my true heart's desire – whether that be a woman or a trip to the tropics – with patience enough to allow Life its surprise curve balls. Curve balls are half the fun, anyway.

That's another way you can recognize a man of heart; he makes most things fun.

2. He laughs easily, authentically

I didn't really know laughter until I was well into my 30s. Oh, I laughed plenty before then. But I took myself and life so seriously that my laughter was shallow and intellectual. Only I didn't know that until the wisdom in my heart started showing me the wild beauty in all things.

Rainer Maria Rilke wrote, *"If your daily life seems poor, do not blame it; blame yourself that you are not poet enough to call forth its riches; for the Creator, there is no poverty."*

My intellect has always been predisposed to lie to me by telling me things are worse than they really are. My brain usually says I've got to work harder, be better and do more just to survive, never mind thrive. It says the same about you. And my balls, well, they're never satisfied for long. It's hard to fully let go and surrender to laughter when I believe I'm still not yet good enough – or that you aren't, or that life isn't.

My heart, on the other hand, is perfectly content to enjoy this moment. It can find the innocence in most any situation, and it can laugh effortlessly at the crazy divine comedy that is life. The heart doesn't laugh in shallow arrogance through a facade of "I'm better and smarter than you."

A man connected to heart knows we're all made of the same stuff underneath the surface gloss. The laughter that erupts from that place is profound, divine. It's like the sound of love tickling itself.

3. He's kind to the world

A man connected to his heart is kind to everyone. That doesn't mean he likes everyone. It doesn't mean he tolerates everyone. He might even put someone in jail if they prove to threaten the world he envisions. But he can always see the innocence that leads to ignorant, even awful behavior.

A man connected to heart can hold compassion for the worst, even as he locks the cell door.

I saw this in my relationships with women who acted in destructive ways because they did not know how to effectively communicate their pain to me. Stuck in my head, I judged and fought them for their immature behavior while ignoring the pain at their core.

With an open heart, I'm more able to stay kind with an intimate partner acting out her pain. And yes, like most things, it's work in progress.

4. He's fully present

I hear this all the time from women, that their men don't seem to be present with them. What does that even mean?

Being fully present is a full-body sport: it requires full participation of the head, the heart AND the balls. When a man lives in his head or his balls alone, his partner won't feel him present. One way that reveals itself is through the quality of his listening.

When I was trapped in the brain-ball matrix, I would only listen to a girlfriend with the singular intent of evaluating to respond. I wanted to keep our thoughts in agreement because that's the only place I figured peace of mind and sex could happen. My attempt to intellectualize every argument however, mostly created chaos.

When a man connected to heart listens, he listens with his entire body (which includes his brain and his balls). He doesn't just listen for a way into the outcome he wants. He listens with his whole body for the deeper message beneath the words. He listens at the level of heart, where the real truth often resides.

His partner can feel this, his presence, when he breaths deeply and listens with his whole body.

5. He's passionately living his true purpose

The work I did in the military felt completely out of alignment with my true purpose. I was miserable. The day I left, I instinctively knew to run fast and run far. Not from the military, but from living inauthentically.

The pain of that situation – where I had money, prestige, comfort, respect, and misery – left me with no choice but to seek my true purpose in life, wherever that journey would take me.

That's why I went through such darkness. To find my path of heart, I had to break the stranglehold my brain and balls had on my heart – they didn't surrender graciously.

A man connected to his heart lives the truth inside that heart, whatever it looks like. If he's doing work he doesn't love, he's doing it for bigger reasons driven by his authentic heart; perhaps to take care of his family or serve his community.

In my case, after years of running from the imaginary security of a paycheck in search of authentic work aligned with my heart's desire, I finally found it in writing and coaching. I'm really good at both, and I make a meaningful difference in people's lives everyday. I would have never come this far if not for the immense power in my heart.

 13

THE HARDEST LIFE LESSON: SELF-LOVE

I still sometimes say "yes" when I deeply want to say "no" (and vice versa) … and then resent others, or life, for my choices.

I still sometimes walk paths that feel heavy because logic says this will get me the love, validation, etc. I want. Which is mostly always wrong.

I've been taught that love, peace, fulfillment, affection, validation, etc. comes from the world around me, and to get it I must dance like a monkey on a chain crashing cute little cymbals together for crackers.

Sure, I get my crackers, dancing like a monkey for others' pleasure.

But I'm tired of crackers!

Where's the Feast?

I am discovering the Feast is in living self-love everyday, regardless where it takes me or what it gets me … in loving and honoring my deeper knowing so completely that I am not willing to move into any experience that feels heavy, regardless what my scarcity-minded, fear-filled ego-brain tells me about it.

Throughout my life, when I've felt compelled to move deeper into some darkness – into heaviness – it always turned out that I needed to learn something massive for my evolution … and suffering is a great teacher!

I'm done suffering intentionally for the sake of "growth."

My current practice is self-love.

It's perhaps the hardest practice – and often the most terrifying, too, for it threatens everything we've been taught about how to get love and acceptance (from the outside world).

But I ache for the Feast.

So my moment-to-moment practice is to honor what is deeply true for me by speaking, walking, living, breathing, fully surrendering to my deeper knowing without often knowing why it's true or what it will get me.

Sometimes the practice is just closing the gap between the moment I sell myself out and the moment I adjust by coming back Home to myself.

A big part of this practice is also not making others, or life, dance like a subservient monkey to please, validate, or take care of me, either.

There's another name for practicing self-love everyday:

Letting go.

 14

THE HOPE & HOPELESSNESS OF MODERN ROMANCE

We are deeply disoriented.

Our intimate relationships routinely fluctuate between ecstatic and infuriating. We mostly don't want to live without an intimate partner, yet we can't seem to learn how to really love one either.

We are stuck in a perpetual uncertainty between hope and hopelessness, like monkeys with our hands caught in a coconut trap. We yearn for the sweet fruit inside that we'll never get to taste because the trapper is coming for our heads, and yet we can't let go.

But why should it be any other way?

No one ever teaches us how to do this wild dance of intimacy. Most of us learn from watching our parents just winging it, which for most of us speaks volumes as to why we are so confused. It's common understanding, even if not quite so simple, that half of all marriages end in divorce. What about the half that stay together? What percentage of that half are genuinely fulfilled by the experience?

In my world, among friends and people I've already worked with in my coaching practice, very few would say they want their parents' relationship. Many recognize that what their parents created is no model for a loving, thoughtful, and truly fulfilling relationship.

What's worse, as we look into the world around us, we see examples of men and women not knowing how to genuinely love and appreciate each other. Throughout the world, in politics, education, industry, economics, ecology, athletics and more, the feminine contributions of nurturing, collaboration, and genuine heart-revealing vulnerability, are not much embraced.

Actually, they're mostly ridiculed.

Why Women Often Hate Themselves

A strong woman friend of mine today said, *"I really don't understand why so many women seem to hate themselves."*

Yet how could they otherwise? The world teaches women to hate themselves. The world teaches women (and also men) to hate feminine expression, that it has no productive value to society.

We worship masculine modes of human expression: competition, productivity, accomplishment, shows of strength, intellect, problem-solving, individualism. We depreciate feminine modes of expression: collaboration, relatedness, holistic care and nurturing, emotional wisdom, compassion, creativity (that isn't merely used for profit).

Thus we live in a world literally driving itself to emotional sickness and exhaustion. What hope do we have when the world continues to deny half its very soul?

A New Hope

Actually, I believe we have tremendous hope.

I believe we stand on the cliff of tremendous change in human behavior dynamics. Women's issues are taking front stage all over the world. Yes, women are still being targeted and treated as property to be exploited everywhere. But global awareness of this tragic imbalance is increasing like never before.

The gradual rise of Western Woman to prominence in our communities, while still very much an evolution in process, is forcing the modern world to reconsider a woman's role in human civilization.

Romance

Romance only began to appear at large in the human experience in the 12th Century, during the so-called dark ages when worship of any Feminine Deities was considered blasphemy punishable by death. For millennia women were to be treated as property and utility to serve masculine ambitions. Any acknowledgement of a Divine Feminine principle was driven underground, where it flourished with religious sects such as the Cathars in southern Europe (who were brutally destroyed during the Inquisition). Such worship of the Feminine would resurface in the medieval courts of Kings and Queens as noble warriors known as Knights "courted" maidens, not to have sex with but to be inspired by in battle. The tale of Sir Lancelot and Guinevere is an example of this courtly love taken too far, to the ruin of King and Kingdom.

In our modern age, passionate romance is perhaps the only arena of human experience in which we are forced to surrender our rational thoughts and planned-out lives to the whimsical feminine mysteries of love. Like Lancelot and Guinever, and King Arthur alongside, our tidy planned out worlds are suddenly thrown into disarray when Love arrives.

Romance shocks the logical mind and thrusts us into the blissful ecstasy of union between our masculine and feminine souls.

It's like grabbing an electrical wire with wet hands. No wonder we mostly suck at it. Who ever gets good at holding onto electrical wires?

A Poetic Vision To Live For

I grew up watching 4 parents – mom, dad, step-dad, and stepmom – make messy relationships. Judging by my own disastrous intimate relationships throughout my 20s and 30s, I clearly didn't learn much helpful from them.

But I am now learning. A lot. My life's work is now about teaching people the art of masculine-feminine dynamics – particularly in the dance of intimate relationship.

There is hope for humanity. I believe romance is a critical part of our path forward. It's the most extraordinary container the modern world knows in which the masculine and feminine aspects of our soul can finally be fused together.

The only question is whether they come together in an opposing clash of forces to create an awful supernova explosion; or whether they flow together in exquisite harmony, exchanging their complementary forces to create a power source more brilliant than the sun.

I know that sounds poetic. I'm a romantic at heart. I genuinely see that extraordinary relationships – and a thriving human civilization – are only possible once we're willing to embrace both masculine and feminine ways of being in our own bodies and in the world around us.

That's a poetic vision worth living for.

 **15**

FIND A GREAT RELATIONSHIP (BY COMMITTING TO BEING SINGLE)

I'm single. Committed single.

Until life drops an exquisite woman onto my path with whom it is just undeniable to the core of my being that this is the woman I was born to create worlds with.

But I get this question a lot: *"Why aren't you in a relationship now?"*

Why? Because being coupled up makes me no more inherently valuable and worthy as a human being than being single.

I'm happy with my single status life.

Curious that no one ever asks when you're happy in relationship, *"Why aren't you single?"*

Anyway, relationship is only a pathway to our profound awakening, and by "relationship" I mean RELATIONSHIP TO EVERYTHING:

Relationship to money, sex, career, mom and dad, friends, animals, the planet, intimate partners – all these relationships can serve to surface our limiting, fear-based thoughts and how we play small and sell out our deepest heart yearnings for the empty promises of security. Seeing our fear-based thoughts through the mirroring of relationships can allow us to finally heal those stressful mental programs. Which I recommend to anyone who wants to wake the hell up from insanity!

The most important relationship of all is to yourself.

If you can't untangle that messy relationship with yourself and learn to find the love already overflowing deep within you … well, an intimate relationship is likely then to be disappointing. Because your partner ain't gonna show up with a love you can't find in yourself.

So I'm committed single until committing to relationship is a clear "Hell Yes!"

In the meantime, I keep doing the worthy work of coming home to myself, creating an awesome life everyday.

When that sexy, delicious other finally shows up and my soul reaches out through my heart to wrap her up safe in my embrace, I'll be filled with so much goddamn love she can't help but get it all over her precious self.

That's why I'm not in a relationship now.

**4 months after I wrote this, I met the most exquisite woman I've been waiting a lifetime for. We're engaged now, so take this to heart!

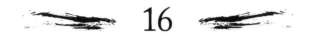 16

YOU DO NOT SERVE ANYONE BY SHRINKING YOURSELF FOR LOVE

Woman, I know you have been hearing for a lifetime that you're too much: too needy, too loud, too opinionated, too demanding, too happy, too sad, too large, too emotional, too expressive, too whatever. So you learned to shrink yourself in countless ways, to disappear or somehow deny your true full expression as a woman.

Which only always then makes you somehow not enough. It's tragic. You can't win. So why not stop trying? Please hear this:

You do not serve a man by shrinking yourself to fit inside his limited capacity to love you. You cannot scare off a man – or anyone – who is genuinely ready to learn how to love all of you. You're perfect as you are.

Which doesn't mean you don't have your own inner work to do. Of course you do, we all, men and woman, act unskillfully out of fear and old false-self limiting beliefs that just push love away.

But never forget that you're here to express the fullness of you, moment by moment, from your agony to your ecstasy.

If you really are too much for someone – and you will know because they'll be constantly fighting to shrink you into something they can understand and manage or they'll just keep running away – then you do not serve that someone by shrinking yourself just to keep them close.

Anyway, why would you want to be with someone who keeps showing you they aren't at least willing to learn how to love you?

You aren't here to just be easy to put up with.

A man truly worthy of your heart is one who is willing to show up and fight whatever dragons arise inside him that disconnect him from his heart and prevent him from offering his love.

Look, none of us have been taught how to love. Actually we've been taught the opposite. We've been taught that logic and reason – especially our own – should take priority over emotions and feelings which are just obstacles to progress and productivity, which is why we dismiss you when you don't act the way we want you to (which is only almost always).

It's your willingness, your courage, to offer all of you, even the uncomfortable parts, that is our invitation to get out of our heads and drop into our hearts.

If a man is clearly committed to resisting the fullness of you, don't suffer yourself till he figures it out. Let him resist and let him go. Letting him go just might be the wakeup call he needs to figure out he's only here to learn how to love, anyway!

And if he is genuinely ready to love you, he'll be willing to fight those fire-breathing dragons that guard the gates to his heart. For that's the only way he can ever claim the massive treasures hidden inside yours.

We need you awake and alive and lit up in the fullness of you. Don't shrink yourself just to get love. You didn't come here to play small in love. You didn't come here to enable others to play small in love, either.

You are humanity's invitation back into heart.

 17

"I DON'T WANT DRAMA" (BEWARE THE MAN WHO SAYS THIS)

Have you encountered the man (or been that man) who emphatically claims, *"I don't want drama!"*?

Swipe right – or left, I don't know – whichever way you swipe to pass on someone you don't want to date, swipe that way because pass on this man you must!

"I don't want drama" is what the perpetually confused and frustrated man puts on his dating profile – or repeats in conversation and often with a fair amount of drama in his own voice – who is nonetheless irresistibly drawn to women with whom he will co-create "drama" until he is one day finally willing to learn how to embrace the fullness of a woman, and the fullness of life itself.

When a man says *"I don't want drama,"* he is essentially saying, *"I am terrified of feeling out of control, and I cannot be with anyone who feels feelings or acts in ways that are beyond my current capacity to feel or simply outside my tiny stress-free comfort zone."*

Which means he will inevitably reject any woman who feels more than he does or who acts in ways that aren't easy for him to be with, which is pretty much every woman, and certainly the women he will be drawn to.

That's the nature of life itself.

For every man, in his deepest heart, aches to be held accountable to showing up fully in his life, and fully for love. Actually, a man *requires* an intimate partner who challenges and inspires him to grow everyday more into his masterful self.

Of course, every man yearns for an intimate partner who loves him profoundly despite his imperfections, one who can consistently see through his human flaws to the very best of him.

But no man genuinely wants an intimate partner who will just let him get away with living and loving small, with playing safe in his own life such that he contents himself to easy paths where nothing meaningful is ever at stake. Which is why a man will often stop choosing a woman who stops challenging him because she's stopped being true to herself and her own wants, desires, needs.

In other words, no man truly wants to live anything less than his full potential as a deep-souled human being who is every day committed to giving his greatest gifts to the planet, to his community, to his family, and to his intimate partner.

Whether or not he is conscious of it, a man needs a partner who will challenge him. Challenge is the only thing that inspires a strong, masculine-identified man to rise into becoming his best self every day.

I'm not saying every man responds so well to a challenging partner. Of course not! Many men clearly don't. Many men choose a perfectly challenging partner and then soon lament their choice. He'll even blame her for making his life more difficult, all the while ignorant of or just in outright denial of the fact that he is choosing this experience! But only because no one teaches us men why we would actually choose – can *only* choose – a partner who indeed challenges us.

To be sure, there are countless unskillful ways that women challenge adult men that can cause even the most self-aware of men to drive that "no drama" stake deeper into the ground. So I encourage anyone who wishes to partner with a strong man to learn skillful ways of offering him the more wild and unruly passions of your authentic heart. In other words, you can learn how to challenge him with love, with respect, rather than merely mirror his "no-drama" neediness with your "emotional connection-at-any-cost" neediness.

Nonetheless, always remember this:

Until a man can just embrace that a partner who lovingly challenges him is what he requires to help him live into his mastery as a truly powerful, authentic, heart-centered man, he will continue his futile quest for that mythical woman who is both mysterious and alluring enough that he wants to have sex with her, *and* who will somehow give him "no drama."

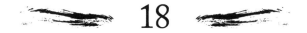

18

A MAN WITHOUT A FATHER'S PRAISE (NEVER FEELS SUCCESSFUL ENOUGH)

"The more fragile a man feels internally,
the more likely he is to try building an outer shell to hide this fragility."
– Guy Corneau (Absent Fathers Lost Sons)

Throughout my life I have been plagued by the enduring fear that I'm n*ever quite successful enough*, whatever my actual successes. Which has been at times a kind of torture for every woman I ever tried to love.

For I have tragically sacrificed love, over and over again, on the raging pyres of an endless (and futile) pursuit of some "ultimate success" that nonetheless refuses to reveal itself. No matter how bright the burn of my sacrificial fires, that final success I've hunted has only ever persisted to lurk stubborn in the dark shadows just beyond light's edge.

I know now it wasn't some ultimate external success I was seeking, but rather the enduring and unassailable peace-of-mind I hoped it would bring.

Since diving deep into men's inner growth work a decade ago, and through coaching hundreds of other men along the way, I've discovered a profound connection between the enduring absence of a man's peace-of-mind and the enduring absence of praise from a father, or any male-elder's praise.

A Boy Without A Man's Presence

My dad mostly stopped paying attention to me when I was 4 years old. Not because he was somehow a bad father. That was simply my age when he and my mom ended their turbulent marriage, and he moved out, and mostly on, forever.

Though he stayed in touch and I saw him occasionally throughout my youth, the immense void of his daily presence brought with it an immense absence of masculine-energy guidance and praise from an elder man – the very thing a boy requires to become a man, himself.

"A man who 'cannot get it together' is a man who has probably not had the opportunity to undergo ritual initiation into the deep structures of manhood. He remains a boy – not because he wants to, but because no one has shown him the way to transform his boy energies into man energies."
– Moore & Gillette (King Warrior Lover Magician)

Like so many grown men who remain psychologically adolescent well into adulthood, throughout my 20s, 30s, even into my 40s, I ached deeply for a wise elder man's guidance, for his blessing and benediction into my own manhood.

I just never knew it. I wouldn't have admitted it, anyway, so angry was I at being left alone (by men) to find my own way.

For when a boy grows up without the consistent presence of an elder male father-like figure, he grows up believing he's on his own (a physically present but emotionally distant or abusive man is not "present" for the boy). A wise elder woman (e.g. mom), no matter how loving, can't show a boy the way into becoming a mature man. She can surely teach him many essential things – like how a woman expects to be treated by a man – but she can't model manhood for him, *not in the body*, where he most needs to learn about "Being Man."

When I was 10, two curious events happened that clearly reveal the affect of his absence on me, emotionally, physically, mentally, and the life-long consequences that followed.

The first happened at a soccer game.

While I played in hundreds of organized sports league games throughout my youth, my dad only came to two.

Both were disasters.

In soccer, I'd been a star forward, one of the highest scorers in the league.

Until the day my dad showed up.

On that day, acutely aware my absent father was watching me from the sidelines, I suddenly felt as though my body had been unplugged from some cosmic electrical socket, as all the energy had been drained from my 10-year old body.

During a climactic moment on the field, with the ball at my feet, the goal suddenly opened up before me. Instead of striking a decisive rocket-shot into the back of the net, my limp little legs could barely muster a weak toe-tap to the ball, which sent it rolling gently, timidly, along the ground towards the goalie, who scooped it up easily, like he was simply picking up his pet.

I'd never felt so viscerally incapacitated, physically incapable of "success."

The second disaster happened at a baseball game.

I was the starting pitcher that day. Dad showed up and volunteered to be home plate umpire, as dads may do at their kids' games. I took the mound and looked towards home plate, where I saw my absent father's eyes staring directly back at me from behind the shadowy black grill of the umpire's mask.

This time he was no mere spectator. He was specifically charged with judging my every toss of the ball in his direction: Did I throw a good pitch (success) or a bad one (failure)? My dad alone would decide, and the game (and my fragile masculine-worthiness) would hang in his balance.

Again I felt paralyzed, the electrical umbilical cord supplying energy to my boy-body ripped from its source. Instead of fastballs straight over the plate, my listless pitching arm could only offer soft, high arcing lobs that soared high over the heads of both batter and father-judge.

A few pitches in, dad stopped the game, flipped up his mask of menace and asked for help from both coaches. He didn't know how to call my softball pitches in this baseball game.

I don't recall whether my dad reassured and praised me at either game. He may have. What I do recall, viscerally, was my shame at failing to perform. I also recall an overwhelming sadness at knowing he wouldn't likely attend any more games.

I didn't openly express my emotions on either day. I didn't know how. Yet my impotent performance revealed it all.

It's just … no one was present enough to notice.

Since then there was never a convincing voice in my head reassuring me I'm a successful man, a worthy man. Women would often reassure me I'm a "good man," yet that was never suitable substitute for the blessing of a wise, trustable elder man.

A boy can only receive meaningful affirmation of his Manhood from the Men already wholly living inside their own.

Thus was my journey, like so many men, that in the absence of an elder man's wisdom and guidance I too often felt rudderless, powerless, lost adrift in the vast oceans of my life, unable to feel deeply successful for more than rare fleeting moments.

Without a better model of manhood, I naturally defaulted to popular culture's half-baked ideals: A "Real Man" is a moneymaker who dominates on the field, in the bedroom and the boardroom, whose only permissible emotion is anger, which he uses to get his way.

But I didn't trust these shallow ideals. Few men genuinely do. Most of us see them as faint shadows, at best, of far more profound and expansive truths about our nature.

So while I looked outwardly successful – money, woman, impact – I felt utterly unworthy of it all, endlessly hungry, always craving for more.

Without a wise elder man (that I trusted) regularly reassuring me that I'm inherently successful – good enough, loved, worthy as I am, regardless the size of my bank account or number of notches on my bedpost or whether I win or lose – I only knew to keep seeking fulfillment by exploiting the world around me.

Which is the best way to never finding fulfillment.

For when one can't feel successful within their own being, no external accomplishment would ever satisfy.

When one can't generate true generosity within their own thoughts, they'll always see strings attached to the generosity of others.

When one can't connect to the profound love in their own heart, they won't trust the love of anyone else.

Lack of Masculine Fulfillment Destroys Intimacy

Without the capacity to feel deeply successful, loved, and worthy of love, my intimate partnerships suffered greatly.

For when a woman dared express upset towards me in some moment of her hurting, she was rarely met with my empathy and understanding. Instead, she would suddenly find herself pressed right up against the cold stone walls of my indifference and anger, built strong and sky-high to keep hidden (mostly from myself) my deep reservoirs of confusion, sadness, and shame.

I also regularly subjected every woman I ever loved – including my current partner at our start – to the inevitable suffering that comes with loving a man whose insatiable need for external success can drive him to pursue "opportunities" that don't serve the relationship, and may outright harm it.

Yet how could it have been any other way?

I was living in the near-complete absence of an elder man's voice reassuring me that I'm inherently a success in his eyes.

No woman or accomplishment can ever substitute for the blessing into manhood that can only come from wiser, elder men. It isn't an intimate partner's role to bestow upon a man the measure of his internal worth.

It is an elder's guidance and praise that can put his mind at ease, whatever his circumstances. Even if that elder be dead, or not his actual father, it's the praising, encouraging words of a trustable elder man's voice resounding through his head that can finally calm his otherwise restless spirit.

(Side note: You may find it curious, as I do, that the "God" of many modern religions, while generally seen as a loving "Father," nonetheless demands "His children" daily prove their worthiness to be with him, forever casting those who fail into some awful abyss of perpetual suffering. Sounds suspiciously a lot like many human fathers!)

At age 38 I attended a weekend initiatory rite of passage experience for men. Shortly after arriving, I was led to a chair at the edge of a woods, where I sat before a white-haired elder man I'd never met.

He looked me in the eyes and said only these words:

"Welcome. We have been waiting for you a long time."

Now, for all I knew of this mystery man, he could have been an absolute wreck of a human. Nonetheless, I began to weep.

His simple, heartfelt words were gently whispering to a great yearning in my soul. Whoever he be, this elder was giving witness to my profound exhaustion at carrying a terrible burden of aloneness for a lifetime. His words reassured me I was no longer alone, that I was being embraced, welcomed home, even though I'd never been to these woods before. This stranger man pierced me with a sentence I hadn't even known I needed to hear.

My own father seems incapable of offering me this gift. We speak from time to time, and I know him as a good-hearted man. But I wouldn't even trust such words from his mouth, for I realized (decided) long ago he was simply as lost as a Man as I was. He didn't grow up feeling supported and encouraged by men, either.

The Essential (Paradoxical) Role of Father

The essential role of "father" in a child's life, particularly for boy, is a paradox. He must challenge him such that he learns to stand his own ground and find his own place in the world, yet also simultaneously guide and reassure him such that he lives in the direction of ideals worthy of his heart, his being as a Man.

It's a delicate dance few of our fathers ever did well (though I believe this is now slowly changing).

Many of us are intimately familiar with the challenges laid down by a father (or by other boys/men), through competition, comparison, criticism. Which is why we endlessly strive to achieve, to win, to exploit the world around us, whatever the cost. In that world, winning is our only shot at safety.

Few of us also regularly received reassurance and genuinely helpful wisdom from our fathers. Thus we wear our masks of invincibility, insisting we know what we're doing, despite feeling painfully lost all the while.

I believe humanity will be transformed by fathers learning to say more often to their children (whatever their gender), *"I love you. You are already a magnificent success in my eyes."*

For those of us men (and women) who are destined to live essentially without that voice in this lifetime, it falls upon us then to find that voice within ourselves all the same – to re-parent ourselves, you could say. The crux of my own deepest, most difficult (internal) work for the last two decades has been "switching on" my own internal voice of reassurance and worthiness.

By confronting my hidden rage, my enduring sadness, I've allowed myself to grieve my absent father. Through years of inner mindset work, I've learned to overthrow the ignorant critic within when he rises to insist nothing I do is enough.

I've finally initiated my own wise, inner elder who daily reassures me I am "walking success," and that my simple presence is the greatest gift I can ever give to anyone. Hearing these words, even if only in my own head, calms me in a way little else ever can, including money and measurable success.

Every man must discover for himself that there's no form of external success – not money, career, sex, or relationship – that can fill the father-sized hole in his heart. He must undertake the (inner) journey of learning how to lift and fill himself up in ways that don't merely depend on his external circumstances.

The depth and quality of his life, and his relationships to others, to his intimate partner and especially to himself, fully depends on it.

 19

THERE'S NO
BAD TIMING FOR LOVE
(WHEN YOU'RE TRULY READY)

More and more I'm convinced the success of intimate relationship strongly depends on *timing*.

I don't mean perfect accidental timing, like where you just happen to be at the post office on the exact day, at the precise hour, minute, second that The One needs stamps.

I don't mean bad circumstantial timing, like your co-worker crush finally confesses to their mutual crush a week before you're leaving for a new job in Asia.

No, I mean internal developmental-stage timing, as in you are genuinely, deeply ready, no matter your external circumstances, to both receive the vast riches and lean into the intense rigors that come with any truly worthwhile intimate relationship.

Many people *say* they are ready, but they're just not. I thought I was ready in my 20s. I thought I was ready in my 30s. But the disastrous results I repeatedly experienced as I tried again and again to do committed relationship with a human woman, revealed that I was in fact not ready. From the perch I sit upon today, I see clearly that I was not genuinely, deeply, *unwaveringly* ready for a committed intimate relationship until my early 40s.

Even then, upon meeting the extraordinary woman I'd waited a lifetime for, I would soon face difficult challenges for which I did not feel prepared, and sometimes felt still unwilling to face, and so almost walked away from. But I was finally, truly ready for intimacy with another human – and so was my partner – which is why we made it through.

For many people, this is what I've discovered "I'm ready" means:

"I'm ready for someone to give me everything I dream of having – all the love, sex, affection, validation, good times, and whatever else I want from romance. I am sooo ready for all that!"

That's not "ready" for intimate relationship – not with another actual human person, anyway. That's adolescent fairy-tale fantasy refusing to grow up.

Being truly ready for intimate relationship means more than getting your needs and wants met. Surely certain needs and wants must get met to have a healthy experience.

But make no mistake: Being truly ready also means being willing, now and forevermore, to stare down and best the ugly dragons that live inside you. Because the one you've been waiting for will also likely be "the one with both the maps and the keys to the dark, dank dungeons where you keep those dragons hidden and locked away."

They'll also have the willingness, maybe even the desire, to unleash those dragons to wreak havoc within you whenever you resist offering your love out of some ego-centric fear that doesn't serve anyone.

In other words, true intimacy will require of you the endless, and sometimes excruciating, inner work of removing obstacles that prevent you from more fully opening of your heart. This is no quick journey for the faint of heart, but a lifetime adventure for the courageously willing.

Relationship is your heart-work forever in progress. No one outside you will ever "complete" you. No one is going to show up with giant palm fronds to fan you and silver trays filled for years with all those juicy, plump grapes you crave, despite the promises of your fantasy.

You're already complete, with or without a partner.

You're a living, breathing cosmic progeny of this infinite Universe, born at the leading edge of all creation! Whatever in creation's name has caused you to believe the story that you need something outside yourself to be complete has been lying to you.

Until you get that – at least intellectually, if not in your bones – you will endlessly, unconsciously, seek outside your own heart for a "bigger, better deal" than what you now have. Which will be an ongoing nightmare for you and your partner, particularly if they, too, are endlessly seeking a "bigger, better deal" outside themselves (and if you are, then they surely are, for you are indeed mirrors of each other).

In other words, you'll just end up blaming your person for the havoc caused by your own dragons, and you'll eventually have to replace them with a new person you (foolishly) hope won't discover you have any.

So, consider that "good timing" just means you're finally ready to make an outrageous, courageous stand for love.

Love is messy.

Love is challenging.

Yet how else can we expand our capacity to love if not for life's messy challenges that force us to confront the limitations of our loving?

Beware: Until you are willing to fully face the challenges and embrace the messy, you won't be truly ready for intimate relationship – your "timing" will somehow always just seem *off.*

Note: This is NOT advocacy for staying in abusive or unhealthy relationships in which your partner ain't willing to grow. I'm a huge fan of learning to keep your heart open even as you walk out the door to exit an unhealthy situation.

 20

THE 3 STAGES OF LOVE (WHERE ARE YOU?)

I'm a huge fan of disillusionment.

Having an illusion ripped away from us can be profoundly liberating. Dorothy had to discover the Wizard of Oz was just a conman before she could discover she already had the power to get herself home.

When it comes to love, disillusionment is essential, if also profoundly painful. It's also inevitable. For there's a core reason why our relationships and … well, our entire lives, really, are so fraught with struggle and heartache:

We're looking for love in all the wrong places.

We spend most of our lives looking for love outside ourselves, expecting other people, circumstances, experiences, to give it to us. Eventually we realize – if we're lucky – that love from outside sources is completely unreliable. Other people inevitably disappoint us, let us down, change in ways we don't want them to, or simply leave. Sometimes they leave mentally or emotionally even when they stay physically.

I once married a French woman only five weeks after we met. I was fresh out of the military and felt completely disconnected from my heart. The day we married on a pristine sunset beach in South Florida, my heart already knew what my head refused to accept: this love adventure was going to destroy me.

I expected this luscious French woman to love me in all the right ways. Pretty quickly, though, she proved she wouldn't love me in any of the ways I really wanted! She wouldn't kiss me good morning. She wouldn't scratch my back. She wouldn't let me spoon her at night. She would play with the dogs and not me when she came home from work. She wouldn't even make love to me for most of the 8 months we were together; we didn't even have sex during our epic honeymoon adventure in Mallorca, Spain! Disillusionment hit me like a 105-pound French woman with a cigarette and an attitude!

Here's the real gift she gave me: She woke me up to how poorly I loved.

The moment she didn't give me what I wanted, I immediately found a way to withdraw my love from her: I'd get upset, complain about her behavior, check out emotionally, stop doing things for her, even threaten to leave. I thought *she* was the nightmare. Turns out, I was!

This experience was a genesis for perhaps my biggest life lesson:

The only way to lasting fulfillment in relationship is by offering my love freely without expecting anything in return for it.

Which brings me to the Three Stages of Love. Which stage you live in affects the quality, depth and magic of your experiences in life and love.

Stage 1 – "I *need you* to love/need me."

In Stage 1, I need the outside world to appreciate me, validate me, respect me, love me. To experience love, I need the outside world to be a certain way. My parents have to approve of me. I need to make this much money. My girlfriend has to behave in ways I like. My friends have to treat me a certain way.

Oh my, what an unstable existence!

Love just evaporates the moment the world stops meeting our conditions! If we can avoid cynicism, eventually we simply realize Stage 1 love isn't reliable. It's completely ephemeral, and thus not consistently fulfilling.

This hurts too much. Disillusionment sets in.

Welcome to Stage 2.

Stage 2 – "I will love myself."

I don't need you to love me. I'll give love to myself. I'll take myself on dates and vacations. I'll pamper myself with good food and clothes and trips to the spa. In fact, I'll do something awesome for me everyday. I'll meditate and do yoga, maybe go find myself in India. I'll be kind to me and say affirmations in the mirror about how wonderful, beautiful, brilliant and delicious I am! I'll say to myself, "I love you!" and I might even marry myself (self-marriage ceremonies are now in fashion).

I'll develop both my masculine and feminine qualities so that I am a whole, complete individual. My life is more or less great with or without a partner. Not needing a partner feels really empowering to me, and safe.

Before long, though, I realize that safety becomes stagnant, maybe even suffocating. Although I love myself consistently which feels nice, I only give love to others when it's appropriate and feels good, because I know they're responsible for their own self-love, too. I also don't fully accept another person's love because I know it's unstable.

Something is missing. Disillusionment is stirring.

Welcome to Stage 3.

Stage 3 – "I *am* Love, itself."

I have discovered an endless well-spring of love sourced deep within my very own heart. I can radiate love into the world because I now know I could never possibly run out! Effortlessly, I give love to myself and my partner, to bored workers at the DMV, to democrats and republicans, to the whole world. I still work towards a better world, but no longer with anxiety. I have finally learned to love everything this crazy life throws at me.

I instinctively move away from people who want to hurt me because I love myself deeply. Where I used to leave in anger, now I leave in love because I know only people in pain want others to hurt, too. Still, I'll love them from a distance.

I'm free to live my authentic truth everyday. I don't need validation from outside me.

Disillusionment is welcome, because I know it just points the way towards a deeper love within me that doesn't depend on outside conditions.

If I have a partner, I love her with all of me, always curious to explore how I might make her life richer. She's free to show up however she wants, because I simply love doing this exquisite dance with her. We're also both free to end this dance whenever we feel that's our deepest truth.

We simply let love show the way.

Note: Though my thoughts on this were originally inspired by David Deida's 3 Stages model, my interpretation is my own and not intended to represent his work.

PART 2

DANCING
IN THE FIRE

 21

BREATHING INTO (UNTIMELY) SEXUAL ENERGY

Sexual energy rises and falls in the body like the tides.

I'm a single man, living in Santa Monica, California, surrounded by brilliant AND gorgeous women. Yet I have no intimate female partner with whom I can express the natural sexual energies coursing through my body every single damn day. Do you have any idea how often the intoxicating magnetism of a feminine woman's physical presence attempts to seduce me?

An attractive, feminine woman is like a brilliant full moon shining resplendent over the ocean of my masculine sexuality. I'm literally pulled towards her like gravity.

Here's basically what happens:

In the presence of an attractive woman relaxed in her feminine being, I may initially feel a delicious, thick energy alight deep inside me – depending on the woman and the moment, it may simply start in my groin. If the chemistry quickens, that energy spark will rapidly expand outward to fill my entire body with heat, pressing impatiently against my skin like a storm-raging river threatening to overwhelm its banks. In this state, the urge to release this expanding energy through any kind of physical contact is immense, even if that means taking care of it myself. If I stay with this energy in the presence of the woman, my focus instinctively narrows until

I'm a hungry tiger creeping through tall grass towards a lone, unsuspecting wildebeest taking sun on the Savannah. I don't just want to devour her … I *need* to.

This is where the intellectual battle begins.

My awareness of the larger social context crashes into my primal desire to ravish and penetrate her (not just physically, but emotionally, psychologically, spiritually). There is absolutely nothing like holistically ravishing a woman when the stars are aligned in support of that adventure. However, in most cases, I'm clear that a sexual interaction with the woman before me is NOT the best choice for either of us.

Does this happen to you, too?

The essential question is wtf do I do with all that delicious sexual energy when I know I shouldn't externally express it, and I definitely don't want to internally castrate it?!

The only reason a man or woman can't be authentic friends with the sex of their attraction is because they haven't yet learned how to JUST BE with their sexual energy and not feel compelled to do something (anything!) about it.

No one ever taught me how to simply be with my sexual energy.

Did anyone teach you?

Culture has conditioned me to believe I must either sex, masturbate, shame or numb it away. I learned early that a real man gets his prey (i.e. has lots of sex, no matter how he does so), while a lesser man loses out and masturbates the tension away. The shameful man stunts that sexual energy by berating himself for feeling anything in the first place. And the man who numbs it away with rationalization, work, alcohol, TV, etc. … well, umm … I'm sorry, remind me what is this man living for again?

I've been all four at one time or another.

These days, I am fortunate to have many amazing female friends. If I were to routinely indulge the strong sexual energy coursing through me, I would surely create much chaos in my personal relationships ... just before losing them. I don't want that. Nor do I want to numb or shame my sexuality away or masturbate myself to sleep every night.

Fortunately, I'm discovering another way.

BREATHE INTO IT – The Wisdom Within The Fire

On my recent "30-Day Sex, Dating, Flirting, Hunting & Hoping Diet" I started learning to sit in the experience of my fiery sexual energy without having to do anything about it.

In my mindfulness project for military veterans, Operation Mindful Warrior (I'm a military vet), our foundational mindfulness practice is to ask yourself, "What am I experiencing right now?" and then notice all the thoughts and physical body sensations happening in this moment and to simply breathe into all that.

We take 3 deep breaths, consciously allowing any internal bedlam to settle like flakes falling faintly to the bottom of a snow globe.

By just consciously breathing into that intoxicating sexual gravity, I can relax my quickening thoughts for a moment to discern whether all the stars are aligned for a soul-satisfying sensual experience, or whether the Tiger just wants to be fed.

In other words, mindful breathing helps me wade through the wild energies stirring within to find the clarity of what Life (as opposed to my lizard brain) is really calling for in this moment. Naturally, there are times when outward expression is clearly what Life wants right now. But if I'm not consciously breathing, all I see is the passionate heat expanding inside my skin that wants to explode into her, consequences be damned! The result is typically either inappropriate external expression or deadening internal castration.

Three deep breaths helps me discern the true wisdom within the fire.

Conscious breathing also helps me circulate that sexual energy through my whole body so that it doesn't get stuck or hastily evacuated.

The payoff is that I can be fully present with an attractive woman and deeply nurture the trust, respect and intimacy required of a beautiful friendship. And I love beautiful friendships. Should that warm sexual energy ever surge through me, I can simply allow myself to relish it fully, without compulsion, without shame.

Unless I notice the stars winking in our direction. In which case I'll take one exquisite, deep breath ... and swim spirited towards the moon.

It's essential to have a simple, useful practice that helps you move with your own delicious if untimely sexual energy in ways that serve you, rather than merely further wound or starve you.

22

RELATIONSHIPS BETWEEN HUMANS ARE MESSY

We tend to think a "healthy relationship" is one in which we never fight, upset and anger never happen, disagreements are few, the sex is always great, and life together just flows easy like a spring breeze.

That's just rotten baloney.

A genuinely healthy, thriving relationship is one that welcomes the entire human experience, from the sublime to the profane to the downright messy. A genuinely healthy relationship is one in which:

— You learn to not blame each other for your own internal discomforts, but rather are engaged everyday in discovering how to be partners in healing stubborn old wounds.

— Anger and sadness are (mostly) as welcome as joy and enthusiasm.

— Sex is an ongoing exploration fueled by the artful mixing of boundary respect and generous curiosity.

— Anxiety and insecurity are not dismissed as signs that anyone is broken or weak, but instead are handled with deep reverence and loving care (for that's how they may heal).

— You learn that disagreement doesn't have to end you, but can actually help you create an exciting new world of delightful possibilities neither of you can create alone.

— You discover that learning how to give your partner what they seem to need most from you — and what you most resist giving — is exactly what is required for your own healing.

— You realize your partner's upsets and hurts can be a direct pathway for connecting to your own heart.

— You are gifted with unending opportunities to discover the limitations to your loving that are merely unconscious projections of your own fears and wounds onto your beloved's being.

— You are also gifted with unending opportunities to discover where are the necessary limits of your healthy boundaries such that you may continue to not just survive your life, but deeply thrive in it.

Do you see? You're human. Being human is messy. A relationship is the coming together of two humans! Humans coming together is messy! (take that however you will)

Relationships indeed will not always be clean, easy, or harmonious. They are the expression of two distinct thought-worlds smashing into each other, separate planets suddenly fusing into one entirely new celestial body.

You think there isn't going to be some fire and chaos and confusion and doubt and even utter destruction of the precious realities you've long held as true in your old safe little world? There will indeed be fire and confusion! The world you've known is coming to an end. Now you're learning to live on this new planet that isn't even done forming itself. It's never done forming.

Like any living thing, a relationship is always evolving, changing, endlessly cycling from life to death back to life on its march towards infinity. Of course you're going to feel disoriented and destabilized, even completely lost sometimes.

At times you'll probably even hate this new world you're creating with this other human. It's unfamiliar, the rules are different here, and the natives don't always (or even often) behave or think in ways you'd expect. Some part of you will probably always want to escape this new planet, too, thinking there's another planet much more hospitable to your way of life ... somewhere out there!

Though if you do rocket off this strange planet, you'll only land somewhere else where the same physics apply. You live in a human universe. You cannot escape yourself.

Be gentle as you collide in relationship with another human. You can rest assured that if either of you knew how to do it better, you would absolutely do it better. No one (with a conscience) goes into a relationship thinking, *"I can't wait to screw up this person's life!"*

If your relationship isn't at least a bit messy and disorienting at times, you're probably exerting way too much effort in trying to control the collision. The key is learning how to embrace the mess – even enjoy getting it all over you – for then intimate relationship becomes the most exquisite pathway for your most profound life transformation.

A PRACTICE

Take a few moments and simply forgive yourself, and your partner (past or present), for all the unskillful, thoughtless, insensitive, even ridiculous behavior you (and they) have offered up in the exquisite, fiery collision of intimate relating.

Take more than a few deep breaths and notice how delightfully absurd it all is – always wanting to do better, be better, feel better, love better, and be loved better, and yet nonetheless still somehow (too often) experiencing something less than the complete fulfillment of your yearning heart.

 *23*

STOP TRYING TO CONVINCE ANYONE OF ANYTHING

The most significant intimate relationship through the first 20 years of my adult life, which cut deep into my 30s, was also the craziest. By "craziest" I just mean we made each other daily insane.

We took each other into the darkest, most absurd realms of insecure, aggressive, and offensive conversation that neither of us could have imagined we'd ever encounter in "romantic" relationship. Although I do give us credit for stopping short of actually killing each other, sometimes I wonder how close we were. It was downright excruciating at times.

However, through that experience I also learned an incredibly liberating distinction:

I don't ever have to convince anyone of anything about me, or about anything else, for that matter.

Never mind our childish verbal communication, you should have seen the ridiculously long emails, endlessly scrolling text messages, and rapid-fire Facebook posts we would throw back and forth at each other. I, meticulous practitioner of the art of communication, would lay out my every essential, nuanced point in numbered bullet format with key phrases bolded or italicized, sentences scrubbed over and over for clarity and brevity, each word carefully chosen to ensure one desired outcome: that she finally "get" exactly whatever it was I was desperately wanting her to get.

Sound familiar?

Of course, at best her responses would perplex me and suggest she'd barely read what I so carefully wrote. At worst she would respond as if I'd sent her only a photo of a giant middle-finger wearing a fuck-you bow-tie.

Either way, she'd only ever come back to re-assert her original position on whatever imagined upset of the moment we were both in uproar about, though clearly for different (imagined) reasons. To which I, now armed with even deeper certainty of my righteousness, would once again launch into some fresh reshaping of my perspective, believing THIS time it would finally fit in her throat as I worked to thrust my certainty down into her being with scant mercy.

Thus we washed each other with mud, rinsed off with glue, and repeated for about 5 years.

Why was I so desperate to make her think like me? Actually, I know why. She criticized me a lot, and somewhere deep inside I believed in her criticism, and it hurt. If I could only get her to stop and see me in a different light, then I believed I wouldn't hurt inside anymore.

I didn't realize the only person that really needed to stop criticizing me was … me.

Her words hurt me because, inside, I believed them. If I didn't they couldn't possibly have hurt. Sure, it might have been disappointing that this woman I wanted to love so deeply couldn't see the brilliant, innocent child of the universe that I actually am – that we all are. But at least I wouldn't have taken it so personally. I would have understood she was just having a nightmare and that no amount of my impassioned protesting was going to awaken her from an illusion she wasn't much willing to examine. (Much later I would also learn, as you'll discover in this book, that there was so much more to her upsets that I was missing, and that she was aching for me to see, however unskillful her attempts)

By taking her on and resisting her world view, by working so passionately to change it, I only gave the hurt more power. What we resist indeed persists. I proved it over and over in that relationship.

Since learning that lesson, it's been among the most liberating experiences of my life to simply allow people whatever viewpoints they choose to believe in.

Admittedly, it's a work in progress. When I believe passionately in a thought, an idea, a perspective or a story, and I simply think it's "right" I can be tempted to fight for its survival if I think someone is threatening to invalidate it. I turn into a fundamentalist thought-savor willing to employ any measure to prevent my idea from extinction at the hands of some thought-poacher hunting in ignorance.

But that's just more insane thinking at play.

It's actually the easiest thing in the world to let someone else think whatever they want to think. What do I really gain when someone agrees with or validates me? A good feeling? I can feel good regardless whether anyone agrees with me.

It doesn't mean I have to hang around and stay in the conversation. Although I'll never know for sure, I'm confident one of these two scenarios would have played out had I simply stopped trying to constantly take her perspectives away from her: She would have eventually grown weary of hearing herself repeatedly tell the same negative stories about me and shifted naturally to see me in a different light; or I would have simply stopped resonating with the negative tone of our daily conversations and left years before I finally did.

But at that time I needed to stay in there and battle it out for one reason: she was bringing me face to face with my deepest fears about myself. She gave me the opportunity to explore and ultimately discover that all those negative, critical thoughts I also believed about myself, well, that they just weren't true.

It was one of the greatest gifts she ever gave me. Because now I realize I don't have to convince anyone of anything. I'm only ever trying to convince myself, anyway. I'm not perfect. I still mess up sometimes. I'm human just like everyone else and still have to work at consistently living an authentic life with heart-centered intentions. But I don't have to convince anyone that I'm worthy of respect, kindness, consideration, and love; that I'm essentially an innocent child of this Universe consistently doing the best I know to do. I don't have to defend what I think or make anyone think like me.

If someone doesn't resonate with who they believe I am … well, isn't it just the most delicious thing in the world to be with people who genuinely appreciate you for who you are today?

That's what I'm calling into my life. And the only way I'll do that is to stop trying to convince anyone of anything.

A PRACTICE

If you ever find yourself trying to convince someone of something – whether partner, family member, friend, or co-worker – when suddenly you find your head swirling in stress, your palms sweating and voice agitated, and you realize you would gladly trade your good health for earplugs, a vodka, and a large mallet (to beat the walls, of course, not the person in front of you), try this experiment:

1. Stop talking.

Bring your attention into your body. Can you notice feelings of stress or tension or panic anywhere in your body? Do you feel tightness or heaviness? Do you notice feelings of anger? Sadness? Despair? Frustration? Is your heart beating fast? Are you experiencing a desire to flee, attack, or freeze? Do none of that. Take a deep breath instead.

2. Ask yourself, *"Is it really so important that this person agree with me?"*

What would do you think you'll get if they do? Validation? Proof of your intelligence, your value, or your worthiness? A good feeling?

3. Give all that – validation, sense of worthiness, good feelings – to yourself.

You don't need anyone's permission to think what you think or to feel good about yourself. What is the worst that could happen if you simply let them think what they think?

Even if you disagree on a sensitive issue, they'll likely appreciate you and feel safe in your presence all the more, if you simply give them the space to believe whatever they want to believe. Even if it's something they believe about you. The only thing you have to lose is your attachment to other people's thoughts.

What do you stand to gain? Only your sanity, inner freedom, joy, enthusiasm, and a peace of mind that doesn't depend on what anyone else thinks about you.

If you do find yourself regularly struggling to convince someone in your life to see the world – or you – in a different light, how's that working out? What might happen if you simply give them the space to think whatever they may think? What do you think you're saving them from? Or yourself?

 24

CAN I WALK YOU TO YOUR CAR?

"Can I walk you to your car?" I asked her.

"Oh, don't worry, I can walk myself," she responded.

The boy inside me thought, yeah, she can walk herself; she doesn't need me.

The Man inside me thought, yes, she can walk herself, and I will walk her, anyway, so long as I'm confident she doesn't feel actually threatened by me.

It was dark outside, a bit after 11pm in this quiet Santa Monica neighborhood. Probably safe. But you never know. I had just spoken at an event in a friend's home about a personal story of transformation and how to step deeper into the challenges Life is calling forth from each of us.

I met this delightful woman shortly after my presentation and we laughed most of the rest of the night together. At one point during the evening, someone convinced us to swap shirts in the middle of my friend's living room, a challenge we gladly took on while surrounded by amused others (she had an undershirt on and so remained fully covered during the swap, though I did not, and thus I did not). Her dainty white shirt wrapped itself tight around me like a cotton torso Speedo, my forearms bulging out of its elastic sleeve cuffs like sausage being squeezed out of a plastic wrapper. My silver embroidered Japanese koi T-shirt draped her tiny frame like a petite woman in a man's T-shirt. She looked good. I was told I looked like either a pirate or a young, gay-ish Bradley Cooper. Whatever. I was thoroughly enjoying the presence of this playful feminine woman.

The Man in me asked to see her again soon.

The boy in me whispered I wasn't Man enough.

"Where is your car?" I asked as everyone was leaving.

"Oh, just right around the corner … somewhere over … mmmm… there-ish."

"Ok, I'll walk you," the Man in me told her, sensing her uncertainty in the darkened street.

"No, really, you don't have to. I'll be ok. I'm from Jersey!" … said the *man inside her.*

The boy inside me eagerly agreed I didn't have to. He actually thought I shouldn't, anyway, since she clearly communicated she didn't need my presence. I'm probably just gonna make her more uncomfortable by insisting, and the boy inside me has always been mortified to impose upon a woman. Better to let her walk the dark streets alone than risk imposing my presence upon her. I'm sure her car is close, even if neither of us can see it.

The Man inside me said, *"Nonsense. I'm here."*

"She'll be more safe if I walk her to her car than if I don't. She may not know or fully trust me yet. And while that may be wise of her … I know me. She will be safe with me. I'm just walking her to her car. I'm not asking anything of her other than to allow me to help ensure she gets safely on her way."

As a Man in this moment that alone is my sacred duty. I want only to keep her safe … even from me.

Where is the line?

She told me at least twice I did not need to walk her. She wasn't upset about my insistence. We had good rapport going, and I believed she instinctively trusted me, but should I have let her walk alone?

A lady friend I shared this story with today told me that many women in our culture are taught two things: (a) to be independent and not need men, and (b) to not inconvenience a man.

I don't know what was at play for this woman. I did notice that as she expressed not to need me, lots of internal programming implored me to back off and let her walk herself into an unnecessarily risky situation.

The boy in me urged me to let her go, mostly from fear of her rejection, but also for fear of not wanting to make her uncomfortable in any way. The Man in me wouldn't hear of it, knowing the risk she was taking if I didn't step up despite her assurances.

I'd like to think that had she really been committed to refusing my presence, she would have made it unmistakably clear and I would have backed off and let her go to whatever fate awaited her choice. Which in all likelihood was simply to walk to her car alone at night in the dark with only her thoughts as company. I would have moved on to wherever I was next called (which at that moment was to my home, to write and to rest).

Again, where is that line? Between her resistant assurances and my steadfast presence as a Man committed to making the world more safe for a woman? I know some women would have been deeply offended by my actions, insisting that the first time she said, *"No, thank you,"* was my clear cue to leave her to her own. This is a dilemma many men regularly face.

I do know she got to her car safely. We stood and talked a few minutes in the street, enjoying the full moon while laughing some more about this and that. Finally, we shared a friendly hug and she got in her car.

As I began walking away, she lowered her window and with a grateful smile sent these delicious words floating towards me on a silver moonbeam:

"Thank you for walking me to my car."

"Thank you for letting me wear your shirt," I responded.

We both laughed once more, and she drove off into the night.

 *25*

THE ONE THING WOMEN ARE MOST AFRAID OF IN MEN (IT'S NOT AGGRESSION)

I used to think women were only afraid of aggression in men, in all its forms: anger, rage, physical violence, verbal abuse, sexual aggression, rape.

I grew up with all kinds of conflicting social messages about the wrongs (and subtle rights) of violence against women. With three sisters and two mothers (married to my two fathers), I learned early there was something inherently special about women, that they were different from men not just in body parts, but in essence. I knew they should be protected and respected.

In addition to the daily masculine aggression towards women that I encountered outside my home, I also witnessed an explosive masculine anger inside my home that horrified me and my sisters. Seeing my tiny, frightened sisters routinely recoil in the face of an awful masculine rage only reinforced my ideas about a woman's singular fear.

I learned to loathe the thought of making a woman feel unsafe in my presence. I wanted to make women feel good, to like me, and I had seen how aggression made them not feel good, how it made them hate a man.

So I did my best to never express aggression with a woman.

Even sexually. I shut down sexually towards women for fear that my desire would be interpreted by them as aggression. Throughout my dating life and well into relationships, until I was 100% certain a woman welcomed a next step with me, I would not proceed with a next step. A woman had to practically stick her tongue down my throat before I understood that kissing her was welcome.

I castrated myself in countless ways to protect women from any hint of masculine aggression in me. I often practiced what I believed was the most certain way to make a woman feel safe: I made myself invisible to her.

Whether that meant backing down, staying out of her way, leaving the room, or simply pretending I didn't want to passionately devour her when I so desperately did, I made myself as non-threatening in a woman's presence as I could position myself to be.

I taught myself how to disappear. To save her from what I thought was her primal fear of my aggression.

Here's what was really happening.

In the last few years I've discovered something women fear even more in men than mere aggression. It's something far more common in our everyday world. Something us men even fear in ourselves, though most aren't even conscious we're doing it.

A feminine-core woman is most afraid of her masculine-core man disappearing. She's afraid of him failing to show up for her. Not stepping up. Walking out. Not staying strong and present, particularly when things get a little crazy and confusing.

Her deepest desire is to be deeply cherished. When he leaves, even just emotionally if not physically, she's left completely uncherished.

Aggression is simply the extreme expression of a man not cherishing a woman.

I checked out for years when my women got too emotional for me, especially when they were angry. I thought if they just saw things differently – if they saw things like I see them – everything would be fine. So I tried like mad to convince their minds to shift. Which rarely worked. They weren't waiting to have their intellects adjusted. So I would constantly give up and run, even when I stayed in the room.

If she fought me long enough, eventually I fought back. A feminine-core woman can't out-masculine me. I will win that battle. And I did. Every time. But I really only ever lost. So did she. Heartbreaking how blind I was to what was actually going on.

I realize now she was simply screaming out her fear, desperate for me to step up strong and claim her heart, to let her know without a doubt that I'm here not going anywhere, to simply reassure her deeply that I got her and won't let anything bad happen to her, and that she's safe in my love.

Women weren't just afraid of my aggression. They were afraid of my leaving, which ironically, tragically, I was doing in countless ways often to avoid my own innate aggression which scared me, too.

Had I known this deeper truth, everything would have been different with most every woman I ever attempted to love. Instead, I labeled immature and mean any woman who ever dared share her pain with me in any way less than perfectly communicated. And then I ran off in every direction.

In my 30s, I lost the most important woman in my life because I couldn't stand in the illusory fire of her pain – a pain largely caused by masculine-abandonment in her own past that had nothing to do with me. I was so triggered by her pain – and particularly the hurtful ways in which she expressed it, which thus caught me up in my own – that I couldn't reassure her that I loved her and would hold her safe as she learned to trust again. I lost her because I couldn't see what was really happening, what she was really asking of me.

She was asking me to step up and fight for her heart.

Fight what? Fight myself. Fight my desire to run. To check out. To disappear. She was begging me to be aggressive with my own inner demons, and perhaps hers, too, in the battle for her sacred feminine heart.

I lost that battle, and not long after our turbulent relationship ended she met the man she would later marry. I continued to grieve that loss even as she had a child with that man, who knew how to show up in ways I still yet had to learn.

Oh what fine messes of hearts I helped create over the years. I didn't know. I'm so sorry. Please forgive me. I see now. I'm growing up. I'm a Man. Eager to share what I've learned through so much pain, with other men who don't yet see, but who are ready to.

I'm finally ready to step up and fight for a woman's heart.

26

YOU CANT BE KING... UNTIL YOU EMBRACE FEMININE ENERGY

No man can truly be King until he is willing to take responsibility not just for himself, but for the entire world around him. Until then, he might get rich, but all he'll have is money.

Last night, I watched the recent remake of "King Arthur" with my lady and my step-father, all cozied up on a couch with 2 Bernese Mountain Dogs and our little Golden Yellowjhan, fireplace crackling in the background.

You probably haven't seen it. I'd heard it was not very good.

But we wanted to watch something all 3 of us could enjoy. My step-father is that classic man's man: He loves action, particularly battle scenes where lots of men kill each other. Silvy loves period pieces and stories of emotional intrigue. I love expansive epics.

This one seemed to have all 3 … and it was fascinating!

It has everything you need to know about the evolution of The Masculine from boy to King, why most men get stuck in perpetual adolescence, and how truly powerful we – man or woman – become when we finally learn to embrace Feminine energy.

King Arthur is the story of a boy who does all he can to avoid his destiny. He has a good heart, defending those close to him with vigor, but the rest of the world? He's far more preoccupied with accumulating wealth and living unnoticed by the bigger powers that would destroy him, that are already destroying the rest of the world.

In other words, like many men today – including myself in many ways – he stubbornly resists taking any real responsibility for what lives beyond his own self-serving concerns.

And there's no wise elder men present to show him how.

One day, a good wizard shows up to guide him towards his destiny.

This wizard is a woman … naturally.

Naturally, he resists and mocks her, even after she saves his life.

So what does this mysterious Feminine muse do to get him to wake up?

She sets upon him all kinds of terrible experiences – confrontations with Death – which he must survive so he may finally be worthy of his birthright as King.

"Not all of him can live," she says as we see him desperately fighting off giant rats and monster-fanged snakes.

Of course not. No man can become the King he was born to be so long as his frightened inner adolescent who refuses to grow up remains in control.

This is why women test the men they love, over and over and over. Not necessarily consciously. Very rarely skillfully. Still, she refuses to be "easy" for him to "deal with." After all, how can she know if a man is truly oriented towards Love if he isn't pushed beyond the limits of his own logic?

That's the Great Gift of the Feminine most men – and most women, too – fail to grasp: She orients us towards Love.

When we refuse to embrace Her influence in our lives, we orient towards shit that doesn't matter: money, orgasm, self-inflation.

Did you see Wonder Woman?

My favorite scene is on the battlefield where the "good guys" have taken Wonder Woman to accomplish their shared mission of stopping the enemy and saving all humanity. In a dirty trench she meets a suffering woman who tells of her village's impending demise just 100 yards away, across a heavily defended front. The men insist on pulling away from this woman, to keep her focused on the "larger mission" as they understand it.

"We can't help these people. We must continue on our mission. You can't go onto that battlefield; you'll get killed. It's no man's land," they say.

Isn't that the lament of so many men?

Intimate relationships are indeed, for so many men, "No Man's Land."

Last summer, I started creating a new online program to help men navigate their specific challenges of relationship. I was calling it "No Man's Land." I put it aside because it felt heavy even for me to continue (Silvy didn't feel thrilled about it, either, most unflattered was she by my insistence that intimate relationship is heavy for men).

Most men's self-worth is tied to performance. If he does good, he is good. Yet so many of us experience relationships as a world in which we're damned if we do, damned if we don't. No matter what we do we can't make – or keep – a woman happy, at least not for long. Seems she's inevitably upset about something we did or didn't do.

Rather than learn to embrace her capricious ways as an ongoing invitation to every day continue pursuing her heart, which is how a relationship stays dynamic and sexy, we take it as an affront to our masculine identity.

This awful misunderstanding is at the core of so much relationship dysfunction and ultimate breakdown.

Wonder Woman waves off the men's objections on that battlefield, insisting that *this* woman and *this* village right in front of them *is* her mission. She charges fearlessly off into No Man's Land as the men naturally look on in horror, afraid of death, her's and their's.

As they watch her successfully make her way through, they're stirred with courage and hope and finally choose to follow her. Naturally, it turns out their mission to save humanity is ultimately fulfilled by following Her lead.

In real relationships, too many men refuse to follow their women onto that battlefield. We hide in the trenches instead, where we think we're safe from death, though we're actually just dying slowly, unfulfilled, as the war grinds on and no connections to the "other side" are ever made.

Yet every ancient boyhood to manhood ritual involves somehow facing and overcoming the fear of Death. I have coached so many men who had everything – wealth, comfort, success – and yet were dead inside because they weren't willing to let it all go to serve something deeper: Love.

In other words, they weren't willing – didn't even know how – to die for Love.

I used to think "Masculine" meant "Leader." (I was in the Air Force.) A few years ago, while on sacred retreat to the Australian Outback with a woman coach I was working with, I had a massive epiphany:

The Feminine uses Her connection to the mysterious heart of life to orient the Masculine towards Love. The Masculine then uses His gifts to figure out how to bring Love into actual Being.

Any other dynamic is a perversion of life.

In the movies, the differences between the good King and the bad King – or the protagonist and the antagonist – are always the same.

A good King is oriented towards Love. He (or she) uses wit and might to restore the world in love, and he welcomes being influenced by others, usually some form of group council.

A bad King is oriented towards his own greed. He'll destroy the world, even everything he cares about, to pursue power for power's sake. He is influenceable by nobody. He demands absolute loyalty from everyone to his own whim.

In King Arthur, the bad King first kills his own wife and later his own daughter, sacrifices to make himself more powerful so he can defeat the good King and hang onto power.

Every man is routinely faced with the choice to sacrifice Love on the altar of his ambitions.

Sometimes a man's ambition is as simple as wanting to watch the game. He'll quickly reject his partner's bids for connection just to see the next play. I've done it. I don't mean to say a man shouldn't have his space to relax and enjoy watching other men solve made-up problems. He surely should.

I'm only pointing out how easily and routinely we all, men and women, can dismiss love with the roll of an eye.

When King Arthur first defeats a horde of enemies with his magical sword, Excalibur, even the most hardened men at his side are electrified, invigorated, shocked. As they should be, for when Masculine and Feminine energy partner as One we can overcome any obstacle.

The first time it happens he confesses, *"I wasn't controlling the sword. It was controlling me."*

After he has fully faced death and is ready to be King – and this happens when he finally takes full responsibility for restoring life to the entire kingdom, even if it costs his life – he learns to fully wield the power of the sword.

He becomes unstoppable, fusing Masculine strength with Feminine magic. The bad King is easily routed, vibrant life restored to the castle and all the realm.

When men (and many women) start learning to embrace the mysterious Feminine in every human heart, the world will be a vastly different place.

Movies are stories that, at their best, teach us something profound about how to live, how to love. A movie won't speak to your heart if it doesn't say something meaningful about the Masculine embracing the Feminine, together righting the world back to Love.

I can't watch movies anymore without seeing some aspect of all this at play. I see it everywhere actually, in our politics, how businesses work, even in sports and games – in Chess, for example, the King can move only one space at a time. But the Queen, now she's the one you need to look out for, for she goes as far as she wants in any direction she wants.

I see it within every man and woman I work with. I see it in me. If you look closely, you'll see it everywhere, too.

27

WHO SHOULD PAY FOR DINNER?

Have you ever puzzled over who should pay for dinner on a first date?

Back when I was living mostly in the land of 50/50 love, what author David Deida would call a Stage 2 relationship (see my essay on The 3 Stages of Love), I wanted my romantic dates to at least pretend they were willing to foot half the dinner bill. Especially on a first date. This would clue me into a woman's level of independence.

I needed to see a woman reach for her purse as I went for the bill, acting like she had every intention to contribute. Even if her reaching was awkward and hesitant, as if feigning the act, I still appreciated it. It was her way of saying, *"Bryan, I don't expect you to take care of me. I can take care of myself."*

Oh, it just made me swoon!

I don't have to take care of this woman? Be still, my 2nd Stage heart!

I may have let a woman or two (or more) pay on the first date. Perhaps if she had asked me out first, or if she insisted twice. If there was a second date, I silently hoped she'd grab the bill and say, *"I got it!"* I'd let her, too, and feel good about myself for doing so.

Evolving Out of Oppressive Stage 1 Love

In a Stage 2 relationship I want a woman who can fully take care of herself, who doesn't need me any more than I need her, and who doesn't expect me to take care of her in any way. We can exchange love and resources on equal terms as complete, whole individuals who would be just fine without each other. This is bliss to anyone evolving out of an oppressive Stage 1 co-dependent love.

A Stage 1 lover picks up the dinner check out of obligation, a sense of duty, and often as an act of power or manipulation. Such a person usually expects something significant in return, whether gratitude, a kiss, sex, or simply an hour of your time, this person only gives to get.

When a Stage 1 lover doesn't get what they want, they do not give. If you're out to dinner with someone who loves this way, you'll likely feel the weight of their expectation for you to do your part. For example, when a man compliments a woman and gets upset because she doesn't offer the appreciation he wants in return, he's offering Stage 1 love.

A Stage 2 lover, on the other hand, treats you as an equal … as in, the same. They might open the door for you or massage your shoulders for a minute, but they're meeting you on equal ground. They want their shoulders massaged, too, for an equal amount of time, and it's totally cool if you open the door for them, too, and they'll expect you to should you reach the door first.

They also might *not* open the door for you if it would inconvenience them. After all, they're not responsible for you. They don't want you to expect anything from them, and they won't expect anything from you, either – at least they'll try their best not to.

A couple in Stage 2 offers love cautiously to each other, often checking in for agreement along the way. I lived in Stage 2 for most of my life. I thought that's where the magic was. I was wrong. Loving this way eventually made my most significant relationships unsatisfying at best, and horrific at worst. Because we gave cautiously to the relationship and determined to maintain our independence, we were never able to fully surrender in love to each other. We played love safe, splitting every bill both literally and metaphorically speaking.

Modern western culture idolizes safe Stage 2 loving. Understandably so. Eons of oppressive Stage 1 love has created a world in which women's freedoms are repressed and men resent being manipulated by those repressed women. Stage 2 love mostly satisfies on superficial levels. No one takes the risks required to love from the most profound depths.

But let's get back to that first-date dinner.

What Happens When You're Dining With a Stage 3 Companion?

A man loving from Stage 3 will enthusiastically pay the bill when he has the means to pay, and he'll expect nothing in return, not even a "thank you." Paying is his gift, to himself. It's an authentic expression of his capacity to love freely, which feels awesome to him. No matter how his date receives it, he enjoys giving it.

He might still appreciate her offer to pay. A Stage 3 man also wants a woman who can take care of herself. He doesn't want a dependent partner looking for a meal ticket. However, this man is delighted by an independent woman who is actually strong enough to relax and let him take care of her. She has nothing to prove, for she's a Stage 3 woman. She loves giving her authentic gifts, too, and a part of her gift is fully receiving her partner's loving.

Nowadays, I feel alive when I pay for a date. I even get great pleasure feeling my resolve strengthen as I wave off her purse reach with a casual, *"No, I got this."*

The other day, I treated a woman to lunch who surely makes a lot more money than me. It was delightful! As I confidently told her to stop reaching for her purse, she immediately gifted me with her bright radiant smile. Her body visibly relaxed, too, and I felt great knowing that my unconditional offer allowed her to be more comfortable in her body. I helped her feel cherished and cared for, and I felt powerful. In that moment of giving my gift freely without expecting anything in return, I received so much.

Do you see a rule in here about who should pay?

I hope not, because there is no rule. We are evolving towards a liberated future for humankind; there is no place for the rules of our essence-oppressing past.

So, what if a man who gives his love freely has finances tighter than his comfort level? Why shouldn't he accept his date's offer to contribute? Might it even be appropriate that she pay the bill?

A female friend of mine in Los Angeles often paid for meals with a Dutch boyfriend she loved deeply. His work visa was expired and he hadn't found work in months. He was so financially poor he had to ride the city bus for an hour to visit her a few miles away.

But he showed up for her in other ways. He loved her deeply by offering a strong, steady masculine presence. He took care of her in ways that didn't require money, which allowed her to relax in his presence. He returned to Holland after a few months so he could work. She followed him soon after. Today, they're thriving together.

There simply is no fixed rule about who should pay!

If you're evolving/healing out of Stage 1 co-dependence and it nourishes you to split the bill as a self-loving act of standing on your own ground while empowering the other to stand on theirs, then split the bill. If it fills you, man or woman, with genuine joy to see your dinner partner smile and relax as you step up and say, *"I got this!"* then you should pay, man or woman, if you have the means. Because it's a gift you give to yourself.

Either way, if you're a woman, it's perfectly appropriate to offer to contribute when the bill arrives. Just watch closely what happens next. For you're about to discover what kind of lover you're dining with, and what kind of lover you are, too.

 28

WHY MEN CAN'T BE FRIENDS WITH WOMEN THEY'RE ATTRACTED TO (& SOME CAN)

Can a man be friends with a woman he's attracted to?

As a man, myself, I have lived this question thoroughly.

The short answer is simply, Yes.

Yes, mature men can be legitimate, authentic friends with the women they're sexually attracted to. We can work respectfully alongside them, hang out with them, have lunch with them, talk sincere and impartial with them about their boyfriends and husbands and do pretty much anything else we'd do with any other friend. Mature men can experience sexual attraction and still honor healthy boundaries with women.

Mature men can do this.

Mature.

Men.

On the other hand, adolescent boys – and men perpetually stuck in adolescent psychology, which is most men according to countless authors and experts in the fields of psychology and men's developmental work – will have difficulty being honest friends with the women they're attracted to.

To be clear, this essay isn't about a man's ability to shift from an intimate relationship to a friendly one with a woman. That's called a breakup and deserves different consideration.

The question I'm asking is, *"Can men be authentic friends with women they want to sleep with but haven't and won't because those women don't seem interested in sleeping with them?"* (Note: I say *"don't seem interested"* because I'm fairly certain men are biologically programmed to never give up hope, no matter what a woman says or does.)

This essay is about men who, like adolescents new to the sexual experience, haven't yet learned how to move their sexual energy in healthy ways when among attractive women – men at the mercy of attraction which complicates interactions. Unfortunately, so many adult males are stuck in a perpetual adolescence. Some haven't even matured *that* far (any similarities between toddlers and political leaders come to mind)?

Of course many grown men have learned how to be respectful human beings, as well as veritable mature men in various aspects of their lives (such as career and fatherhood), but fewer of us ever really learn how to be mature core-masculine men in relationship to core-feminine women with whom we experience strong sexual attractions.

Most men are stuck in perpetual adolescence because our culture both feeds us a steady diet of and caps off our developmental growth with half-baked ideas about what it means to be a man: Real men win at all costs, make all the important rules, make lots of money, sleep with lots of women, have the biggest dick in the room, don't cry or feel emotions or show weakness, etc. As a result, most adult men are profoundly confused about what it means to be a healthy mature man, whether they admit it or not; of course most can't admit it because that would be a mature thing to do. I have been confused for 20 years, and I never even knew it.

That said, here are "4 aspects of masculine immaturity" that prevent men from being *honest* friends with women they're sexually attracted to:

1. Men have not learned how to be with their sexual energy without having to do something about it.

Just like adolescent boys, most grown men in our culture don't have a clue how to *simply be* with the powerful masculine sexual energy coursing through our bodies. So it owns us.

The basic story culture teaches me from birth is that I was born an uncontrollable ravenous shark in a pool filled with tasty guppies. I was then given two strong conflicting directives: (a) eating guppies is a measure of a man's worth, and (b) try not to hurt any guppies. Then I was left on my own to unravel this dilemma while living inside a sexually charged body ready to pound the bottom out of a boat with every erection.

Since men have long felt unsafe and unsupported in being vulnerable to work openly through the resulting confusion, we cope with the inner turmoil in countless unhealthy ways: We sex it, money it, game it, work it, porn it, drug and alcohol it, TV it, shame it, deny it or anger it into oblivion. By doing so, we live perpetually disoriented, and sometimes a detriment to ourselves, to the women we genuinely love and also to those we don't.

For most of my life, whenever confronted with intense sexual experiences in my body, I would usually choose the easiest of shame, sex, or masturbation as my main options for quickly dealing with it. No one ever taught me how to wield my sexual energy in intentional, respectful ways, how to direct it constructively. Most men never learn this.

As long as a man is owned by his sexual energy, he remains stuck in sexual adolescence. Unfortunately this kind of man is all too common in our world, which drives women on Facebook to post frustrated public denunciations like the recent one a female friend of mine wrote:

"If a man has a penis, he wants to sleep with you. Period. It doesn't matter how old he is."

But when a Man matures by learning how to be intentional with his sexual energy and not slave to it, he embodies the essence of what author Byron Katie wrote:

"Just because a man has an erection doesn't mean he has to do anything with it."

Then he can be friends with an attractive woman. If he chooses to.

2. Men don't know the difference between authentic love, romantic love and sexual energy.

In his book, <u>Intimate Communion</u>, David Deida talks about the three separate elements of the intimate experience: love, romance, and polarity (sexual energy). Like adolescent teens confused about the rich new experiences happening in their bodies, most men still confuse sexual polarity with romantic love.

With such an immature man, you can trace the entire path from lust to love along the contours of a woman's aerodynamic ass. Such lust-love thoughts surely tempt me all the time in the presence of attractive women. They'll even insist I could actually LOVE the woman attached to those long legs walking by. But such thoughts are mostly merely mental leakage from my lizard brain. I've learned not to trust them.

Having lived many years in a man's body, I can tell you it is fascinating to have witnessed my own experience of what felt like love for a woman essentially vanish in the afterglow of a powerful orgasm. It's astonishing – if disturbing – just how quick sex can switch a male mind from the "ocean-deep love" setting to the "kiddie-pool shallow" one.

Why do you think urgent flash-in-the-pan sex often leads to short-lasting flash-in-the-pan relationships? When two people don't give themselves breathing space, time, to discern what's really happening between them, they can't easily see that more often than not that it's only everyday sexual polarity at play, not genuine romantic love.

While genuine romantic love is fairly elusive, men can experience sexual polarity with different women ... every ... single ... day. Polarity attraction happens. Constantly. In the grocery store. At the DMV. In our cars. At the bars. On a plane. In a rocket ship to the stars. We're like polarized magnets walking around bumping into each other everywhere. Of course we're going to feel the pull. But that doesn't mean we have to act on it.

Sadly, many immature men intentionally use this polarity-love confusion to manipulate women into sex. Such immature men help confuse the trust right out of women.

For us to become mature men, we must learn to distinguish this sexual polarity energy from both romantic love and our deeper authentic love. We must stop manipulating women into false romances fueled only by sexual energy. And we must gain some level of mastery around how we ultimately wield that sexual energy. Otherwise it will own us and continue ruining potentially great friendships.

3. Most men do not fully respect the boundaries set by women, because they do not fully respect women.

Adolescent boys and aging toddlers have long made up most of culture's rules. Thus we still don't fully respect most feminine ways of being.

We place high value on immature masculine expressions of competition, rational thinking, control and domination, achievement for achievement's sake, etcetera. We place far less value on the feminine gifts of consensus building, intuition and heart-centered thinking, holistic well-being, beauty for its own sake, emotions and vulnerability. This bias is so fundamental to our world that I hardly need to offer examples to convince you (think politics, business, military and war spending, money-driven popular entertainment, billionaire sports athletes and broke school teachers, paternalistic religions, and on and on).

Until we slumbering men fully honor and understand that feminine wisdom is as essential as masculine wisdom to the healthy functioning of the world, we will not be able to fully respect the boundaries of any hot female friends. We will continue exploiting weakness in their defenses, whether with subtle manipulation or actual violence.

4. Men don't know how to be authentically vulnerable.

Most men don't know how to be with awkward feelings and experiences without having to do something "manly" about them. We believe we are supposed to act on our feelings, even if that means forcibly suppressing or drowning them in addictions. We are compelled to take whatever action will get us most quickly away from our discomfort.

That's why we usually hate it when women cry. We don't know a middle way.

We do not know how to simply be with awkward truths, nor do we know how to express them without playing for an outcome. Because so much of our worth is tied to a woman's approval, being vulnerable is particularly difficult in relationship to women.

Our fragile adolescent egos can't risk external feminine rejection of our authentic inner worlds, which includes our own feminine expression. So we'll be vulnerable and tell women how we feel, but we'll do our best to control the scenario so that we either get what we want in the end or keep them far enough away that they can't possibly reject the real us. Which is how adolescent boys behave.

It's impossible to create genuine friendships without being genuinely vulnerable – whether with a woman or another man.

Imagine a world where Men ...

Imagine a world where Men could differentiate between sexual energy, romance and pure love; and where he could acknowledge this openly, without shame, to the women in his world who would appreciate his honesty.

Imagine a world where Men could breathe into their sexual energy and simply enjoy their own erections without always needing something to be done with them.

Imagine a world where Men fully respected Women and the wisdom they offer.

Imagine a world where Men knew how to be vulnerable with their deepest truths, their joys and their sorrows, and could easily share them with women (and other men) without manipulating for some outcome in the sharing.

Wouldn't the Men in such a world make for incredible friends to women, and spine-tingling intimate partners, too?!

 **29**

WOMEN FEEL UNSAFE
AND IT IS OUR FAULT

"We have to take responsibility for what we are not responsible for."
– Robert Moore

In 2013, I attended a large workshop with 2000-ish people, roughly split between men and women.

One day, the facilitator said to the men: *"Raise your hand if you have felt unsafe at any point during the last week."*

Maybe 5 hands went up, of a thousand men.

Then he asked the same of the women: *"Women, how many of you have felt unsafe at any time during the last week?"*

A thousand female hands shot up, as the men – including me – looked around shocked at the revelation.

Our women feel unsafe, constantly. And, yes, it is the fault of Men. All of us.

I write a lot about masculine awakening, what I'm discovering it means to be a mature healthy masculine man in the 21st century. Women, for the most part, love what I write. They're aching for the mature man my essays describe. Men, though, are sometimes angrily triggered by what I write.

Some feel I'm shaming men; that I'm an anti-man feminist-sympathizing misandrist who blames all men (even the "good" ones) for women's dysfunctions and that I excuse women from all responsibility.

The plain truth is I write because I'm a man who's been disoriented for 20 years. As that realization awakens in me, I look out and see an entire world of disorientated men and women struggling to thrive. But I'm not into shaming men. I'm not into shaming *anybody*.

However, I do believe in taking responsibility for our role in the reality we're living. And the reality we live in is women routinely feel unsafe in our society; they are constantly subject to behavior from men that devalues their worth as human beings with something meaningful to offer the planet beyond male sexual release and motherhood.

Women are unsafe and aggressed upon because so many men are stuck in a perpetual adolescence.

As a male culture, we haven't yet fully achieved the mature experience of our masculine nature. Too many men still demean "girls" by pulling on their pigtails, bullying and hitting them, tricking them into showing their boobs and calling them bad names. They just do it now wearing business suits and NFL uniforms, drinking beer instead of Kool-Aid.

I know many good men don't treat women this way. But it's common enough that the majority of women experience it all the time, from our city streets to college dorms to US Congress.

There's another fascinating reason women routinely feel unsafe:

Too many men haven't learned to connect their innate masculine aggression to their hearts.

I wrote a popular article recently about how I grew up believing women were only afraid of aggression in men, so I suppressed any experience of aggression in myself, especially sexual aggression. I did not want women to ever feel unsafe around me. While this enabled me to cultivate beautiful friendships with women, in disowning the primal aggression inherent in my masculinity, I also left women to fend for themselves in many ways.

I believe we don't stand up for women enough. Culturally. Individually. On TV. At work. In our conversations with other men.

I know the male voice isn't completely missing. I know the men reading this are probably the so-called "good" ones. I'm also one of the good ones, and yet I've stayed quiet knowing certain male acquaintances would act terribly towards women, unconsciously content in knowing at least I wasn't the one acting badly.

The evolved masculine nature can be an aggressive force for good. When connected to heart, the mature masculine essence (which is not just a man thing, as women can express masculine energy, too) fights aggressively for the well-being of all beings inside the kingdom. It protects its charges from the forces of chaos and ruin lurking outside our castle walls.

The mature masculine man (or woman) doesn't disconnect from his innate aggression, nor does he wield it for purely self-serving means. The mature masculine man infuses his aggression with love, using that power to enrich the greater good.

For thousands of years our more "civilized" cultures have been expressing this aggressive aspect of masculine force in overwhelmingly destructive ways, disconnected from heart, as oppressor, denier, abuser, exploiter, conquerer. As this immature Lord of the Flies era continues to play out on a planetary scale, our immature masculine nature runs amok, expressing in abundance the entire range of perverted masculine behaviors that destroy our feminine counterparts, from kidnapping them in African villages to sexualizing them in our offices to beating them up in elevators.

Comedian Louis CK – before he was publicly exposed as yet another man who got off on privately exposing himself to women uninvited – cleverly pointed out that men are the number one threat to women:

WOMAN: *"Yeah, I'll go out with you ... alone ... at night ... I'll get in your car with you, with my little shoulders. 'Hi, where are we going?'*

MAN: *'To your death, statistically.'"*

The classic book on masculine archetypes, <u>King Warrior Magician Lover</u>, is about the evolution in males from the "boy psychology" to "man psychology." The authors say this about man psychology:

"Man psychology ... has perhaps always been a rare thing on our planet. It is certainly a rare thing today. The horrible physical and psychological circumstances under which most human beings have lived most places, most of the time, are staggering. Hostile environments always lead to the stunting, twisting, and mutating of an organism. ... Let us frankly admit the enormous difficulty of our situation, for it is only when we allow ourselves to see the seriousness of any problem and to admit what it is we are up against that we can begin to take appropriate action, action that will be life-enhancing for us and for others."

I'm writing this essay because this morning I spoke with a strong female coaching client of mine in San Francisco who melted into tears relating recent stories of daily harassment at the greedy hands of men. Not just your cliche construction workers, but co-workers, colleagues, men at networking events, and even a casual male friend she didn't trust to have in her home because he was always testing her with his sexual agenda. She's no passive pushover woman who can't handle herself, yet why should she have to "handle herself" in this way at all?

Despite our advanced modern technologies, so many modern men are the modern product of ages of warped and twisted masculine expression.

Fox TV regular, Arthur Aidala, in a recent segment on sexual harassment in Congress, proudly demonstrated his technique for "complementing" women on the street by standing up and clapping as an imaginary woman walked by. He says his "smile success rate" is 90%. My coaching client pointed out – as did Daily Show correspondent Jessica Williams – that women smile because they know if they don't give such a man what he clearly wants (attention, acknowledgment) there's a high likelihood he'll get nasty and call them a cunt. Aidala's "success rate" relies on a woman's survival tactic.

Oh, the woeful ignorance of such men.

I grew up surrounded by women. Throughout my life I have heard their stories, and the stories of my girlfriends and female friends, about the demeaning behavior of male colleagues, bosses, friends, strangers, dates, and even their own intimate partners.

The authors of <u>King Warrior Magician Lover</u> also remind us that we must learn to take responsibility for that which we are not responsible for. It does innocent men no good to simply rest in the comfort of knowing they're not the perpetrators. It is our close male friends, our brothers, our fathers, our sons, and even many of us blind to our own behavior, who are making life distasteful to women on a daily basis. Our joking approval, even our silence, in conversations with each other only perpetuates women's suffering.

I do not wish men shame. I know women demean men, too; they also have their learning and growing up to do.

Still, it's on men to confront our own masculine disorientation, to explore where we are stuck in boy psychology – or trapped in the dark shadow aspects of man psychology, which is to say, living as men disconnected from heart. Our unwillingness to face our own selves, whether or not we're acting in these demoralizing ways to women, keeps our world twisted and stunted, and keeps our women feeling unsafe even in the presence of so many "safe" men.

We must learn to use our innate masculine aggression as a constant force for good, lest we leave our women to fend for themselves in a world that still disrespects them daily. We must study and explore and work authentically with other men to uncover what it means to be mature masculine men.

We must each do the inner work necessary to claim our 21st century Manhood, to create a world for our women in which they can finally feel safe.

 # 30

RELATIONSHIPS DIE
BY A THOUSAND LITTLE CUTS

A harsh word here, a tiny rejection there.

Resistance sets in like plaque where there was once only love-flow. Bodies tighten and hearts close in protective response to perceived offenses, rather than stay open and heart-fully confess vulnerable sensitivities.

After a time, so much subtle internal bleeding from those tiny little cuts overwhelms a relationship's vital organs – laughter, joy, communion, sexual expression, playfulness, kindness – all that beauty begins to diminish as the relationship deepens into crisis.

If not reversed with intentional love-in-action, it can all come undone in a spectacular supernova explosion death … or simply one that grows cold and unresponsive over time, expending all its energy until there's nothing left but a dead wasteland no one can live on.

Moment by moment by moment, a relationship thrives or perishes.

Fortunately, it only takes a kind word, a loving gesture, a refocused thought – in other words, the discipline to see the best in someone even when the worst seems so loud to you – to begin healing all those tiny little cuts.

A PRACTICE

Commit to offering kind words and actions to your partner all week.

If you're single, reflect back on a past relationship and mentally offer kind words to that partner, no matter how awful you think they were. Surely they taught you something about love ... perhaps they taught you how to more fully love yourself (the most important lesson of all).

Notice every time you think a harsh thought about someone today, quickly follow it up with a kind one. Notice how light you start to feel.

 31

A MAN DIVIDED
CAUSES STRESS IN HIS PARTNER

Throughout my 20s and 30s, I often stayed in relationships I was deeply divided about staying in.

My mouth would make promises my bones knew I couldn't keep. Which made life awful for any woman who ever tried to love me.

Today, I'm 3 years into the first relationship I feel internally clear about, which makes all the difference. I've been able to overcome challenges, even potentially catastrophic ones, to preserve beautiful connection with my partner, whereas I couldn't usually get past even trivial trials with past partners.

Which is teaching me an essential lesson:

A man must learn to be honest with himself, every day, whether the life he's now living is the life he really wants. Otherwise he's just torturing himself ... and anyone who tries to love him.

A man deeply divided about his choices can't give the best of himself to whatever he's choosing. If he's divided about the work he does, he won't show up fully or enthusiastically. At best he'll offer disconnected work that won't matter much to anyone, least of all himself. Even if he's successful at it.

When I was a military soldier, I was deeply divided about my mission. So much that I soon hated my life. I felt more and more useless – not just to the military, but to my girlfriend, to the world. Though I succeeded as a soldier and my service ended honorably, on the day I left all I could do was grab a backpack and go aimless walkabout into the world. I was dead inside, with nothing to offer anyone. So I left everything, including that girlfriend.

I was internally divided about her, too. I thought I hid it well during our 2 years together, but she knew.

For when a man is internally divided about his partner, for as long as she (or he) chooses to stay with that man she will endure an awful ache borne of his wishy-washy half-loving. She'll rage in response, even if silently, and the relationship will sour.

He likely won't even see how his divided desire for her contributes to her distress. In my *Love, Sex, Relationship Magic* online course, I teach that the "Feminine Objection" in love is always *"Don't abandon me!"**

In his uncertainty, his partner correctly discerns the threat of his abandonment, which never makes her "easier" to be with.

As her upset grows, he might even blame his own confusion on her being "too difficult to please." He wouldn't be entirely wrong, for any man who begins to believe that nothing he does will truly please his partner eventually doubles down on not even trying.

All the while, he remains blind to how his internal confusion makes loving him frightening for her; ever more so as his uncertainty grows, and she feels it.

Of course, doubt and confusion is inevitable for any man. Our clever minds are always making up stories, crafting fantasies about how life would be better, easier, if only … if only a million things. To be human is to endlessly want more and better.

Being internally clear about work or woman doesn't mean it will always be easy or feel good. There will surely be times when his challenges are too much to bear and the idea of cutting cord and running for calmer hills will have appeal.

But he won't cut and run – at least he won't get far – because the depth of his clarity will soon calm the surface waves of his overwhelm. As he gets his breath back, his deeper clarity will allow him to re-engage his commitments, with even more vigor and depth than before he briefly lost his mind to fantasies of an easier life.

Only vigorous commitment can further a man's authentic work in the world. A man must also learn that only vigorous commitment will ever truly delight his woman.

For most every woman, throughout her life, has experienced being loved then abandoned, used then discarded, in countless ways both fleeting and enduring. It's only by the repeated demonstration of an intimate partner's unwavering commitment to loving her, come what may, that she can finally allow herself to relax and truly open in her loving towards him.

Personally, I didn't experience readiness for this kind of commitment until my early 40s. Which partly explains why I always seemed to make women so mad at me, despite my always best intentions.

Then, one night while on a solo retreat in an Idaho mountain cabin, I finally felt in my bones I was ready to build a world with a woman. I felt it so clear that I spoke my readiness aloud towards a black sky of stars sprinkled like glitter.

I met that woman the next day.

We've had our trying times, but my deep clarity of commitment to making our relationship thrive has helped carry me – carry us – through all of them.

Each man needs to find and honor his own timing. Some will be ready in their 20s, some their 60s, and some will see that internal clarity come and go, repeatedly.

I personally believe it's less about the "right partner" and more about the "right timing" for a man, though perhaps it's both coming together at the same time. I do see for many men, that being divided or unclear about his work – his purpose – can cause deep confusion around relationship, too, even if he's with the most exquisite partner.

There's countless reasons why it took 'till my 40s. I doubt I know half of them, though I do believe one of them was still not being clear in my work. Regardless, failing to acknowledge and honor my internal divisions created awful messes of love, causing such unnecessary suffering, both for me and every woman who tried to love me.

An easy partner who tolerates a man's shallow commitment doesn't make relationship better. All it does it enable him to remain out of integrity with himself, and to love only half-way.

This is why a man must be honest with himself about whether he genuinely wants the life he's living today. Otherwise, his lack of vigor for the challenges he faces will only make life poorer for the one who loves him, and for himself, too.

However, when he is deeply *undivided* in his choosing ... well, little can stop *that* man from consistently creating exquisite experiences for himself and anyone fortunate enough to receive the gift of his undivided presence.

*The Masculine Objection is "Don't Control Me"

 32

MEN NEED
SAFE PLACES TO FEEL
(ANGRY)

This past weekend in the fire-scarred mountain forest north of Los Angeles, I sat on dank earth encrusted by fallen pine-needles and listened to a small group of courageous men spread throughout the woods around me roar out a long-repressed rage that shook the trees ... and I smiled.

For on this men's weekend retreat, I was showing these men a new way to be with their emotions, and thus a new way to resolve conflict.

Before we started this practice – which I call "Anger Yoga" – I told them that if we did this right and some hiker on the trail heard us, they'd be terrified, and they'd run till they found reception and could dial up the police. I figured we had a 50/50 chance of being arrested on this lovely Saturday afternoon in the woods.

I actually hadn't intended to teach "anger yoga" on this retreat. But when conflict arose in the group that morning, as it inevitably does when men first get real with each other, and with themselves, I didn't want them to merely try talking it out.

Although "talking it out" is generally considered the mature way to resolve conflict, I know from years of coaching men (and women and couples, too) that merely talking things out when anger is present often just bypasses the emotion and rarely gets to the root cause of the conflict, which is (mostly) never about what's actually happening in the moment, anyway.

No. We men are Angry. Furious. Enraged.

Our rage has nothing to do with those Republicans or those Democrats. It has nothing to do with the (often) unfair accusations our intimate partners make in their moments of upset. We're not angry because of traffic on the 405, or the boss/spouse who doesn't respect us, or the lack of money in our account, or our sports team sucks this year, or, or, or. No.

We're furious because our fathers long ago left us alone to find our own way, even if they were physically present.

We're frustrated because no one taught us how to truly, fully love a woman, or another man, or ourselves.

We're disheartened because we feel deeply unseen in our efforts, in our always good intentions. We've always felt unseen, misunderstood, unacknowledged, for despite all the good we attempt, it's never considered enough. Not by others, and not by ourselves.

Without elders/fathers telling us we're enough, that we're already a success, how can we ever know?

We're confused because we've been taught money, comfort, success should make us happy … yet it never does. We're also scared, because despite our armor we don't feel safe in the world. We don't feel emotionally safe. To feel what we feel. Especially anger. We've only ever seen anger used to hurt people.

In our deepest hearts, we men don't want to hurt anyone. So, at least initially, we'll hurt ourselves instead by swallowing our anger, pretending we're ok when we're not. As it festers inside, it leaks out sideways in the form of meaningless work, shallow relationships, emotional vacancy, and addiction.

For those of us who can't suppress it long (like myself), like trying to hold a giant beach ball under water when our anger finally explodes outward it launches haphazardly misdirected towards an unsuspecting loved one, the driver who just cut us off, our brother who supports republicans/democrats, or the supermarket cashier who can't push the buttons fast enough.

We men desperately need safe places to feel our emotions. Places where we can be witnessed in those emotions without being judged for them.

For even in our intimate relationships, where we're often asked to share our emotions, when we do, it doesn't often go well. After all, our partners tend to mirror our lack of awareness and skill in this domain.

At the retreat, after these men had spent about 30 minutes rumbling the woods* with their anger, howling out like wolves scattered across the land (a beautiful metaphor one of the men used to describe this primal experience), we came back together and circled up.

I invited any man who wanted to be witnessed in whatever emotions remained, to step into the circle. As they did, one by one, each man allowing himself to be witnessed by the men encircling him, and by the towering regal redwoods encircling us all, while residues of anger lingered, what had become more evident now ... was sadness.

One by one, inside the circle, tightly controlled man-faces trembled as the last vestiges of inner resistance finally gave way to anguished torrents of tears and snot. We took turns holding each other as we cried out lifetimes of sadness together. It was wildly beautiful.

I almost wish we had been arrested, for then I'd get to explain in court, on record, that all we men were doing was expressing emotions, doing no damage to anyone or anything, and that we came to the woods because we have few places, if any, where we can safely express out our rage in ways we won't be judged or arrested for, or where we won't in some way hurt others who themselves likely don't feel safe around anger. But we didn't get arrested.

We continued on with our retreat, our wild masculine hearts now splayed wide open, that morning's conflict eliminated not by men struggling to get agreement over the facts of who did what to whom, but by the heartfelt apologies that floated effortlessly out of men who had just been witnessed in – and witness to – the massive pain, and the massive courage, that lives inside every man's heart.

After all, it's impossible to fight someone else once you discover you're only ever fighting against your own internal resistance to fully feeling what you feel.

Imagine a world in which men – women, too – have safe places to feel our anger. What an invigorated, open-hearted, deeply connected world we would surely be.

*Anger Yoga has 3 main rules: (1) Don't damage others. (2) Don't damage yourself (including pushing yourself too far emotionally). (3) Don't damage the environment. Otherwise, let your emotions have you. Using a timer can help contain the experience, too.

 ## 33

HIDING WEAKNESS KILLS MEN

Most men think we have to do it alone. Bear whatever burden alone.

We don't ask for help. We don't confess our worries, our sadnesses, our confusion, our despair. We don't engage other men in vulnerable conversations, and we sure don't let women know what's really going on inside us—unless we think doing so will get us laid, or admiration, or something.

We don't even tell our intimate partners our deepest truths. Yeah, sure, we hear them say they want the truth. But we don't believe them. One of my close man-friends recently told me he grew up in a home with this core message:

"Always tell us the truth ... and we will NOT be able to handle it."

Somehow I learned that message growing up, too.

You?

Another close friend grew up believing he would be abandoned and essentially die if he told a truth he thought might upset his family. He was sexually molested. He told no one and carried the confusing shame alone into adulthood, and then into his marriage. Although he told his wife about the actual event, he didn't tell her about the unhealthy behaviors he had developed over the years to distract himself from the burden of that memory, notably an addiction to porn and excessive romantic flirtations with women who never knew he was married. His inability to share the depth of his very human challenges nearly sabotaged their marriage when she suddenly found out by looking through his phone.

There's a core cultural message that says men can't ever show weakness.

We can't need to rely on anyone, and we can't make a mistake. If we do, the world will fall apart. Or at least we won't have an honorable place in it anymore. Our partner will leave us. Or they'll no longer respect us, in which case they might as well leave us.

So we grin and bear it. We do it ourselves. We bear our own burdens and don't let anyone else help us carry them. When it gets too heavy, we check out. Run away. Drink it, porn it, fuck it, TV it, work it, war and rage it out. In those check-out moments, even when we stay in the room, we leave our families and our communities to fend for themselves. We send everything to hell, screw the consequences.

That's probably why women outlive men. We slowly kill ourselves with unhealthy behavior. Women don't drive men to an early grave, as comedians would have us believe. We drive ourselves.

At its worst, "grin and bear it" leads men to the gravest act of check-out possible: suicide.

What Anthony Bourdain did. What Robin Williams did. What 22 despairing military veterans will do today, and again tomorrow, and again the next day. What aging NFL football players do to themselves. The same thing many teenage boys do, who die by suicide four times more often than girls. Despite women experiencing higher incidents of depression, men across the planet commit suicide more frequently.

Jimmy Stewart, a defensive back with NFL Football's Saints and Lions teams, who retired and became a family therapist to work with athletes and military personnel suffering from PTSD, told ESPN Magazine,

"The four years I played pro football were some of the most horrendous of my life. I cried alone. I was frightened. I badly needed somebody to talk to, and I know so many guys today who feel the same way ... Players are not committing suicide just because they have CTE [brain injury]. They are committing suicide because they refuse to be vulnerable. CTE can cause symptoms of depression, but it's isolation and invulnerability that causes you to commit suicide."

Throughout human history we humans have been tribal creatures. We have always banded together to protect ourselves, our families and communities, from the threats of the day. Today, in our fast-tech individualistic society that still rewards masculine expression (competitiveness, ambition) over feminine (vulnerability, empathy), male aloneness and isolation is one of the biggest threats we know.

As men whose culture tells us we're supposed to always know what to do next, the fact is we often don't. We're each as clueless as anyone else on this wild miraculous planet. We daily deal with emotions and burdens that are way too big for us to carry alone.

These are not weaknesses we're supposed to manhandle into denial. They are our human realities. Confessing that is as good as place as any to start.

We can be strong men and still not know what to do. We can be strong men and still ask for help. Actually, it takes a stronger man to reach out and ask for help, because that man has to push through his internal masculine resistance to the act of being vulnerable.

We weren't meant to bear the burden of our lives, even our internal lives, alone. We were meant to hunt together, live together, work together, heal together, dance together, suffer together, and grow together. We were meant to thrive together.

Many men nonetheless still feel an awful loneliness even when surrounded by others. Truth most men rarely feel safe confessing our deepest truths, for all kinds of reasons, from cultural programming to social concerns (status and the desire to always look good). Yet the cost of hiding our true selves inevitably becomes too much to bear – as evidenced by suicide and too many men running around trying to fill themselves up with endless external accomplishments that can never ultimately satisfy.

We need to have real conversations, with our partners, with our families, and particularly with other men. In the end, we are each ultimately responsible for whether we choose to allow ourselves to be fully seen, or not.

In the next 24 hours, I invite you to have a real conversation with someone you care about, and whom you believe cares about you. Tell them about your deepest secret fear, and also what you love most about their presence. Get real with someone. Your woman, your man, your family, your community – your own life – may very well depend on it.

One more thing: We don't have to make others do it alone, either.

As thoughtful men, we must also ask ourselves: *"Am I the kind of men others feel safe to fully be their human selves around, too?"*

 34

WE MEN MUST LEARN
HOW TO GRIEVE EVERYTHING
(INCLUDING OUR SINGLE LIVES)

"Everything you have ever done has ended. Life is a prolonged farewell. Grief
is the process that finishes things. The end of grief work is to be born again.
So to live well is to grieve well."

– John Bradshaw (Healing the Shame That Binds You)

In 2010, I spent 12 months in a purple SUV Dodge Durango crisscrossing North America on the most wondrous adventure with five other men, five brilliant musical shamans forever my brothers.

That purple Durango – which anyone not color-blind like me always insisted was blue – held us safe as we made magical memories for ourselves and thousands of others brought together and forever bound by the heart-stirring sounds of this band's immortal music. It brought us to Burning Man, dusty and delighted, three times. Later, as I made the long, difficult journey towards a stable life in Los Angeles, on a few nights when I had nowhere else to go, I slept safely inside her quiet embrace.

For six years that truck was the purple/blue cocoon in which my caterpillar Life was forever transformed and eventually took flight as a writer read by millions, a life coach to men and women across the planet, and life partner to the most exquisite and extraordinary woman I know (that SUV drove me to our first date).

Just a year ago, I sold it when fixing it (again) would finally cost more than it was worth.

At the dealership, as I moved into my new car the things I wanted to keep from the truck – old concert fliers stuffed into cracking backseat pockets, the 4-port phone-charger that kept us all from arguing over who's phone needed charging most, the wooden rolling pin I bought to massage my back after it gave out one night on the road between concerts in Salt Lake City and Portland – a massive tsunami of sadness suddenly welled up inside me, painfully overwhelming my usually calm and placid emotional waters.

It felt like I was ditching an old friend to an uncertain fate at the hands of people who couldn't possibly appreciate his incalculable value. Before I pulled away in my sharp and sensible new Kia hybrid, I sat and gazed upon my old companion for a good while, appreciating, remembering, smiling, crying.

When I got home to Silvy, for the rest of that evening my body was repeatedly rocked with convulsive, tear-drenched waves of unprocessed, as-yet-unfelt grief. To my complete surprise, I was finally grieving what had passed four years ago: The end of our daily brotherhood and the death of our collective dream.

The fact that we men rarely let ourselves grieve – do we even know how? – is one of the most debilitating realities of modern life. Even after events like death, we'll still (mostly) stuff down the pain.

And there is so much to grieve.

A few years ago, I worked with a young couple daily torn apart by the sunset. They surfed most days in Malibu, and each day come sunset the woman inevitably became sad. The day was over, and her body was grieving it. Which infuriated her partner, because in his mind, *"It doesn't make sense why she has to be so goddamn sad about something that happens everyday!"*

I know it doesn't make sense.

Yet we men must learn to grieve our own versions of the setting sun. Our relationships with others is at stake. And also our felt sense – our actual experience of being human – depends on our ability to grieve.

I have a beautiful life. Truly, I am blessed with a beautiful and generously spirited woman, a cozy spacious home, work that I love, countless friends that inspire me, and more.

Yet I ache to live closer to my three sisters, whom I love dearly, and who are irreversibly scattered across the continent. My yearning for that closeness will never be satisfied. Also, my father. He is a good man, and even though our relationship is getting better these days, that does little to quiet the rage inside me that rails against both him and a world that left me alone at age 4 to find my own way into adulthood largely without him present.

I've found that allowing myself to grieve – to feel my anger, and my sadness – helps immensely with any experience of loss, whether significant or mundane.

I've also discovered the transition from single man to partnered-man can benefit from grieving, too, even though the partnership be exquisite.

Grieving not over some perceived loss of freedom because let's be real: *We men don't generally feel that "free" when single, either.*

Real relationship requires that we shed the relatively safe and unburdened one-person system of living for the more intricate challenges of a two-person system where self-concern can no longer be the singular concern of our choices and we must learn to take responsibility for others.

To fully show up for real relationship we must grieve what was before so we can fully let it go from our hearts, and allow ourselves to fully, enthusiastically, embrace the bonded dance of relationship with another. When we don't allow ourselves to grieve, everything suffers.

About a year ago, I called my dad while driving. Silvy was in the car. When we hung up, I felt like I often felt (at that time) after talking with him: disappointed and unseen. Silvy felt me, and told me it was ok to pull over to cry. *"No way,"* I thought. *"We've got somewhere to be."* (it was the grocery store)

My relationship with Silvy suffers when I don't allow myself to grieve. I pretend I'm not hurting when I am deeply hurting, and she feels my lack of emotional integrity, and it hurts her. Because when I don't allow myself to hurt, I don't (can't) allow her to hurt, either. Certainly not for a sunset ... or anything, really.

Our resistance to grieving causes our bodies to calcify around the painful emotions stuck inside. Whether or not I'm aware of it (usually I'm not), my partner surely is, particularly when my emotional stuckness shows up as a cold, shutdown indifference that confuses, even frightens her (*"Where the hell did he just go!?"*).

There is immense power and freedom unleashed through a practice of grieving, which can be as simple as allowing sadness to have you for a time, even a short time, when it arises.

Perhaps it is my age. I've been here over 40 years now, ample time to have lost plenty. Perhaps it is the ever-deepening experiencing of my humanity. Whatever it is, it feels good to grieve, even though it hurts. I feel refreshed, somehow stronger, reinvigorated and ready, fully present for whatever adventures life wants to bring me next.

 ## 35

WHY GREAT SEX IS NEVER ENOUGH

Have you ever been in a relationship where the sex was amazing, but most everything else sucked?

You know, as long as you were physically stuck together, everything was great. Meanwhile outside the bedroom you couldn't agree on much (unless it was to have sex outside the bedroom).

I broiled in the fires of such an experience in my 30s, through five long years of the most significant intimate relationship of my life up until that point. Our sexual chemistry was finger-licking delicious. Always. In five years, we probably had less than a 3-pack of condoms worth of bad sex moments. Even our bad sex was great sex.

With our clothes on, though, we were a disaster. We saw too many things differently, and after a few months together we didn't really trust each other. She was sure I wanted to be with other women (I didn't) and I was sure she was always trying to hurt me emotionally (I still believe she was, but I know now only because she was in a lot of pain herself, and she wanted my empathy, which I knew not how to offer).

When things got too tense, I would run away and she would fight harder, which just made me run farther. I always came back once things calmed down though, in large part because the sex was addictive. I would have never stayed around in all that chaos if the sex wasn't so good. (good thing

I stayed around, too, because that relationship has taught me countless massive lessons that I get to turn around and share with others now)

I was 36 when it ended, and clearly still completely ignorant about how to create a relationship that works. Rather than learning how to make it work well, I only knew how to make it exhausting.

Which brings me to the point: Great sex is never enough.

I know that may already be crazy obvious to many people, particularly the older (more experienced) you are, but it isn't obvious to everyone all the time. It's certainly not obvious to the one who's caught up in a sexually gratifying but turbulent relationship experience.

While our sex was divine, the other 23 hours of our day were stressful. I even had nightmares about us while I slept. I tried everything to make it better: couples therapy, self-help books, personal-growth workshops (together and alone), going to a spiritual church and praying to whomever, running away, staying put, and plenty of other curious things I thought might finally bring us blissfully together on all levels. Nothing worked.

In part because we didn't have all of Dr. Pat Allen's "3 C's of Relationship":

1. Chemistry

Oh, we definitely had that one! At least sexual chemistry. Anytime. Anywhere. Any way. Our bodies just fit. Our pheromones flickered bright and brilliant between us like a Las Vegas light show! Physical chemistry was never a problem. However, we didn't have lifestyle or values chemistry, which you might call …

2. Compatibility

We were missing this one in seriously fundamental ways. Although we had enough compatibility to live in the same apartment, it seems we didn't often live in the same universe.

Here's a simple example: She was very private and hated it when I shared openly with other people what I was struggling with, particularly if it involved our relationship. I was a budding young writer and life coach. Sharing my struggles in service to both learning and teaching was foundational to how I would offer my best service to other people struggling in their own lives. In fact, I often reflect that I could not do the coaching work I love to do today, or write the way I love to write, if I was still in that relationship.

We also didn't share an underlying purpose for intimate relationship. Though I doubt either of us were conscious of our "purpose" for relationship at the time, she was surely more clear that she simply wanted a home, a family, and stability. I hadn't even figured out yet what my living, in general, was for, so my lack of clear commitment to home, family, and stability surely clashed with her clarity, and made us fundamentally incompatible, certainly at that time.

But we also struggled greatly in a third area:

3. Communication

In my coaching work, I'm finding so many couples, even when they have compatibility and chemistry, struggle painfully with communication. While modern culture is trying to teach us how to communicate more effectively with each other, many of us still lack the skills to communicate well.

Further, we rarely explore the differences in how masculine-oriented people and feminine-oriented people communicate. Which is tragic, because that's what intimate relationships essentially are: interactions between the very different expressions of masculine and feminine being (which are independent of sex organs).

People who consistently express more masculine energy (man or woman) tend to communicate more at the level of thoughts and ideas. People who are more feminine-oriented in their expression (man or woman) tend to communicate more at the level of feelings and emotions.

Ignorance of this dynamic causes great strain in relationships. I was always trying to meet her at the logical "level of complaint" while completely missing the emotional body of pain and excitement her words were often pointing at. In other words, I was so intellectually focused on the details of her complaints that I failed to hear her yearning for emotional connection with me. Which ruined us.

I see communication strain regularly among the couples I coach. It's not something we're taught in our masculine-oriented culture, yet it sabotages us constantly. Of course, couples who do have great communication skills are able to navigate through many an inevitable storm.

With only physical chemistry and basic compatibility in the sense that we both lived in the same city, we were largely missing two out of the three C's. Yet without all three – even if you do have two – you don't have a sustainable, or healthy relationship.

If you have good communication and compatibility yet without solid chemistry, you're likely to evolve into passionless friends. If you have good communication and solid chemistry yet without a compatibility that can underpin a life together, you'd better be served by remaining as occasional lovers, meeting in mutual times of convenience, rather than trying to attempt committed partnership.

If you have solid chemistry and deep compatibility, yet you lack communication skills, this is the recipe for either chaos or stagnation. Chaos as you attempt to communicate using every ignorant, unskillful means in your arsenal, and stagnation if you give up communicating altogether and just make do with an occasional good fuck as you cohabitate with each other. Of course, a lack of communication often turns into a lack of chemistry, as we tend not to enjoy having sex with someone we don't feel deeply safe with – and safety is what healthy communication creates.

Great sexual chemistry is wonderful, but it can be so overwhelming that it's easy to overlook compatibility issues or stressful patterns of communication.

Without compatibility and communication, those thrilling bedroom fireworks can set your whole life on fire, leaving you wrecked and distraught and addicted to a physical love with an awful hangover. Or, once the physical novelty wears off, you're left staring at a partner with whom you can't really talk to or do the things you love to do.

Either way, great sex alone just doesn't work out well in the long run.

Can you recall how missing one (or more) of the 3 C's played out in your past relationships? Your current relationship?

 36

WHY EVERY COUPLE
SHOULD BREAK UP

I once experienced the most beautiful breakup.

It happened inside a tiny bathroom in a rental cabin my then girlfriend and I were staying in near Tahoe, California. Well into a severe drought, this normally thriving winter playground had little snow. Which could be a metaphor for our relationship, because it had stopped being a fun playground, too.

After just three months we had left the all-things-dreamy phase and were entering the why-is-this-hard phase. Expectations had started creeping into the relationship like kudzu vine. We were slowly suffocating from lack of loving sunlight.

What happened in that bathroom is simple: We let each other off the hook.

We told the truth about what we were each experiencing in the relationship without making each other wrong or responsible in any way. Then we intentionally gave back to each other the freedom to be whoever we authentically wanted to be. During that hour long conversation we both came clean about how we were struggling and let go any expectations that the other try to ease our struggle. We reclaimed our freedom to effortlessly be.

We also decided to end our intimate relationship. We had both been experiencing incompatibilities in the way we relate to each other that we decided we didn't want to continue moving pushing into. Though we surely could have overcome those challenges had we been committed to doing the work, we both decided that right now neither of us wanted to do that kind of work.

So we set each other free.

Every couple should set each other free. By which I mean tell the truth about what's really going on; share what's working and what's not, without obligating each other to do anything about it.

Obligation is bondage. Obligation is why relationships stagnate, or worse: cause them to implode in a fiery fight of chaos and vitriol. Ensuring an ill-fitting obligation gets met often requires some measure of force, whether passive aggression or outright violence.

Telling our personal truth instead sets everyone free. It sets us both free to stay if we're genuinely called to stay, and it gives us the freedom to leave if our deepest truth is to dance elsewhere.

Despite the provocative title of this essay, I'm actually not suggesting every couple break up and stop seeing each other. I'm not suggesting couples should not hunker down and do the work it takes to create a thriving intimate relationship. That would be silly and simply incorrect of me.

I'm only suggesting that we let our partners off the hook. Perhaps the most destructive element in a relationship is the expectation that my partner will behave different than she genuinely wants to.

In the past, when my relationships were struggling to fly, it's almost certainly because expectations were weighing down the vessel. Either mine or hers, and usually both.

It's perfectly appropriate – healthy, even – to make requests for what we want. But it's futile to obligate our partners to do what they do not authentically want to do: touch us more, touch us less, do things different, see things different, think differently, want different things than they actually want, eat differently, spend their free time differently.

I get it, though. We're scared we won't get our needs met, so we obligate the other person to show up and make it happen. In the process, we enslave a good person. Everyone loses, even when you get what you want.

The best gift I can ever give a partner is my happiness that doesn't depend on her behavior. When I make my partner responsible for my happiness, I'm saddling her with an obligation to be a certain way for my well-being.

I've never met a woman who seemed to enjoy wearing a saddle. I sure don't want to wear one. Even horses don't like wearing a saddle until they've been "broken." I don't want a broken woman.

Consider how deeply my partner can relax when she knows she doesn't have to pretend or force herself to be a certain way just to please me!

A wise woman living in the Australian outback with her beautiful family once told me, *"I knew I had met the man I would marry when I didn't want to change anything about him."*

Your intimate partner isn't your project. When I saw myself starting to think of my girlfriend as a project that needed my fixing, I knew it was time to leave. She deserves a man who will worship her as she is today. She's extraordinary. I wasn't offering her that anymore.

After setting each other free, we stayed together in Tahoe a few more days, and those few days were sublime. We started laughing again; we made scrumptious love and slept warm and cuddled close through the night; we once again shared those intimate knowing looks-without-words like we had countless times before. We connected deeply in our authentic love for each other, without expectations, and were once again able to appreciate each other's authentic presence.

Releasing each other from all expectations was profoundly liberating. We could both breathe again.

 **37**

THANK YOU FOR LEAVING ME

A few weeks ago I awoke from a morning dream in which my girlfriend broke up with me. Later that day, she broke up with me.

We were moving through some rough weather at our 6-month mark; nothing I thought catastrophic. I was sure we'd get through. Then she ended it. I was devastated. I did not see it coming … despite that spooky dream.

I immediately tried to remind myself of my own teachings: no matter how charming and wonderful and delicious a catch you surely are, *your partner may still choose to leave you.*

When I work with couples, I always tell them I can't know if our work will keep them together. It might even facilitate their separation. Life has its own agenda, regardless what any of us have to say about it.

Every relationship lives in this reality. You may not see it coming. You may not understand why. You might know in the deep, gritty cracks of your marrow that it doesn't have to be this way because you're willing to grow and you're certain you can work it all out together … *if … only … they'd stay.*

Yet they leave.

A friend reminded me, *"People don't leave relationships because of their reasons. They leave because they choose to leave."*

He's right. I know so many men and women who have experienced the worst: physical and/or verbal violence; lying and affairs; or they'd simply spent years emotionally and physically disconnected from each other yet still chose to stay and figure it out.

Many such relationships can recover beautifully by persevering through disaster, both partners emerging stronger and more grateful for each other as hearts get stretched (painfully) open and authentic love expands.

Yet many choose to leave promising, even good relationships simply because they feel called to do so. Their reasons may not be extreme or even obvious. They just choose to leave, and your world suddenly feels like the Death Star just lasered it to rocky smithereens.

When a relationship ends that you didn't want to end, it can leave you utterly shattered, cruelly fated to endless sleepless nights agonizing over what went wrong.

Rather than wallow in the sickening futility of it all, here's a powerful healing practice:

Find the gifts in their leaving.

I don't really know why this woman chose to leave. I know we were struggling, but I genuinely believe we could have triumphed through this weather to create something extraordinary together. She didn't feel the same. So, to the exquisite woman who recently broke up with me, I say ...

Thank you for leaving me.

Thank you for helping me remember ... that a woman choosing me does not make me more of a man, nor does her choosing to leave make me less of one.

Thank you for reminding me ... that my sense of self-worth and identity do not come from you or any woman.

Thank you for being a courageous example ... of what it looks likes to follow the truth of your heart even when your mind – and mine, and most everyone else's mind around us – really wanted this to go so differently.

Thank you for reminding me of the futility of fear ... I see even more clearly now that when we shape our choices around fear, intimacy suffers. We literally created our worst fear – the fear of losing each other – by making choices and demands intended to avoid it.

Thank you for reminding me to never take for granted ... the delicious gifts of beauty, sensuality, laughter, tenderness, playfulness, adventure and everything else I find delightful about being in the presence of a woman! I'm so sorry I ever took the gift of you for granted!

Thank you for sometimes overwhelming me ... with the depths of your feeling. When you were willing to show me ALL OF YOU – even though my fighting and running proved I could not yet handle all of you – you revealed the limitations of my loving. You showed me where I still carry old wounds, where fear gets in the way of my loving. I see more clearly today where I can bring softness, kindness and compassion to my inner world, and therefore to the entire world.

Thank you on behalf of the next woman ... who chooses to dance with me, for she will have a man even more surrendered to love, with a richer heart and an even bigger embrace in which she can dance her wild heart.

Thank you on behalf of the entire planet ... because as this rips me open and expands my capacity to hold all of a woman in my love, my capacity to hold the entire world in my love expands, too.

Thank you for not insisting I change to please you ... but instead recognizing that who you wanted me to be is not who I deeply desire to be. I'm so grateful you had the courage to set me free to go ... be ... me.

Thank you for being so amazing ... for holding me, crying with me, reassuring me on the day we said goodbye that life just too often doesn't make any damn sense and all we can do is surrender and trust that life ... love ... knows what it's doing, even when we don't.

Thank you for shattering the armor around my heart so thoroughly ... for unleashing this agony so dreadful that I've too long been stuffing deep into my bones where it could only fester and surely one day rise to kill me. Your leaving stabbed me so deep that this thick, nasty buildup of poison can finally flow free from my body.

Thank you for helping me feel such pain ... that I may have more compassion for others in pain. I'm so profoundly sorry I was not always able to have compassion for your pain.

Thank you for loving me, and for allowing me to love you.

Thank you for being an exquisite, extraordinary woman and giving me the profound thrill of being your dancing partner for this brief, infinitesimally minute flash of time in an infinitely vast and timeless universe! Of all the possibilities of existence that I could have chosen to experience during those six months, I would not have chosen one goddamn thing different.

I wish you well on your journey into infinity. I take you in my heart with me on mine. See you when we get there.

I love you.

Note: We were ultimately separated for 3 excruciating weeks, during which a deeper and never-before-noticed layer of armor around my heart was cracked open. That cracking paved the way for us to get back together and begin to create a new experience, which I share about in the following essay.

 38

SOMETIMES THE BEST GIFT IS LEAVING YOUR PARTNER

Throughout my adult life, no woman ever broke up with me whom I didn't want, or even subtly encourage, to leave.

Nope. I was the one who ended intimate relationships. I was also the one who never fully showed up for those relationships.

I only finally realized this after a woman I deeply loved broke up with me.

Ironically, only 2 weeks before she ended things, I wrote this on Facebook:

"Sometimes the best a woman can do for a man is leave him. Too many men will only wake up by experiencing the total unraveling of everything they hold dear (even if they won't admit to holding anything dear).

If you make it easy for a man to love small, he'll never learn to love any bigger.

It took strong women to pretty much make life hell for me to even begin rousing me from my own masculine slumber. You might ask, especially if you're a man: 'Wake up to what?'

Wake up to what it really means to show up in Love."

Ouch.

The weeks that followed our breakup were devastating.

When she left me I was already a renowned relationship coach and blogger.

I had just launched my *Love, Sex, Relationship Magic* online course to teach the world how to make magic in love. I absolutely believed I had the knowledge and commitment to make beautiful lifelong partnership happen with this woman. I knew it wouldn't always be easy, and that we were going through a rough patch. Still, I was certain we would be fine.

Yet to my utter surprise, she ended it and my world came undone.

Suddenly I couldn't sleep even three hours in a night. I was overwhelmed daily by gut-wrenching pangs of despair and sadness. So much of what I previously thought was so important – work success, my creative voice, various personal freedoms – became entirely meaningless. All the worldly problems I was always trying to figure out and solve simply ceased to matter.

What did magically crystalize in my consciousness during this excruciating cleansing was clarity into the deepest yearning I've ever known:

I realized I wanted more than anything to learn how to truly, fully love this woman.

Just three weeks after she left, we had a serendipitous opportunity to interact. She experience me cracked wide open. I was so melted into my heart by the realization that nothing else truly mattered – not my success, not even my life – except learning how to love this woman in ways she would actually know she was loved.

She also experienced my complete surrender to what was happening; I was willing to let her go if that was still her choice. Within a few days, we were back together and getting on with creating an entirely new relationship.

As a result of those three excruciating weeks apart, I learned perhaps the most profound lesson of my life:

No amount of knowledge or insight will ever be more valuable in relationship than simply learning how to stay in my heart.

When we were apart, I ached for her like a man aches for an amputated arm; I had phantom-girlfriend syndrome. I soon realized that my longing for "her" was actually a projection of my profound desire to BE the massive love living inside my own authentic heart.

As an intellectual man trained by culture to emotionally disconnect, I have long struggled to connect with the massive love that insides my own heart. Naturally, it followed that I also struggled to sustain connection with my intimate partners, too.

My head only always got in the way of love. I always wanted to be right – or at least understand why I wasn't.

When I couldn't intellectually understand my partner's pain, I would shut down, convinced it was something in her thinking that was at fault. With my mind already closed to love, my heart could only follow, and soon I would close to the idea of relationship altogether. I created many a mess this way.

I see now that the true gift of intimate relationship reveals itself only when I'm willing to let everything else be less important than learning how to show up in love – including intellectual understanding and being right.

For a smart man who knows lots of stuff and has had all kinds of material success – yet who has long felt something massive was missing in his life – learning how to consistently show up connected to heart, in relationship with my woman, is proving to be the most exquisite adventure of them all!

Indeed, I see now that as I learn how to fully love all of my woman, I learn how to live more consistently connected to my own authentic heart.

 **39**

IS YOUR RELATIONSHIP EXPERIENCING A 'CRISIS OF CONNECTION'?

A few times a year I offer weekend coaching intensives for well-intentioned couples who have ignorantly and innocently conspired together – in some cases for decades – to create a tragic mess of love.

Not long ago, I worked with a young couple in their 30s. We spent an entire weekend nestled together in a quiet canyon home just outside Los Angeles. They'd only been together 18 months, yet they were already embroiled in an excruciating "crisis of connection."

Intimate relationships only truly work when real connection is given highest priority. Everything else between and around you – sex, finances, work, family (even your kids), friends, lifestyle – must come second, at least most of the time, for intimate love to thrive.

Tragically, most of us get this backwards. We prioritize intellectual disagreements over money or sex or work or lifestyle while our experience of connection gets as much consideration as a cucumber in a candy store. Which is a solid example, because wondering why the hell anyone would sell cucumbers at a candy store is a lot like wondering, *"Why the hell isn't this relationship working when I'm doing everything I can to make it work?!"*

All of us, men and women, have been taught for a lifetime to dismiss the experience of connection in favor of more masculine concerns:

Are we functioning ok?
Do we have enough money?
Is there a point to this conversation?
What's broken that I need to fix?
Is anyone bleeding?

Thus we seek to create functional relationships – in other words, predominantly "masculine" ones – that inevitably suffer from chronic disconnection, and thus fail to thrive. It's like building a big beautiful castle, yet there's little life inside. Sometimes there's even outright war within our own castle walls.

Whatever our dissatisfaction, we tend to believe it's caused by alack of desired outcomes: Not enough sex or affection, too much fighting or focusing on the negatives, not enough freedom to be me, or not enough intimacy, though we rarely question what that means.

We fail to realize that these missing outcomes are often the result of a "crisis of connection."

Did you know women initiate 70% of divorces? (ref: American Sociological Association, 2016) Naturally!

The feminine value is connection, and connection is the most consistently overlooked need that both men and women need. It's just that most women feel disconnect, *viscerally*, more than most men.

Even in my relationship, my fiancé usually feels any disconnect between us long before I do. I'll think everything is great – mostly because she doesn't seem upset and no one is bleeding – and suddenly she'll say in sad tones, *"I haven't felt very connected to you lately."*

"What the f*k are you talking about?" … is what I'll think but do my damn best to not say out loud or show on my face because I know better than to immediately reject or invalidate her experience, which would only further her experience of disconnect!

Most women's sensitivity to connection is biologically greater than most men's. With vastly more oxytocin and estrogen, hormones that promote bonding and feeling, most women are literally living in different experiential realities than most men. Higher levels of testosterone cause men to be more action-outcome oriented (*"Is there a point to this conversation?"*) and feel less (*"How do I feel? Ok."*).

Unfortunately, many women don't have skills to effectively communicate their experience in ways that men can really hear, and most men don't have skills to listen beneath the details for what their partners are really asking for.

As we continue to prioritize masculine notions of relationship success, so our "crisis of connection" only deepens.

I've worked with many functioning couples, who even had gorgeous homes and great wealth, who nonetheless lived together in relative misery, sometimes quietly, sometimes painfully out loud.

Such was the case with Stan and Sonya, the couple I hosted for this private weekend intensive. (not their real names)

When a man initiates couples coaching with me, it's quite often because his partner finally made it unmistakably clear that she's done, if she hasn't already walked out. When Stan reached out to me, they were beyond the edge of collapse, already living apart.

Nonetheless, they both showed up. For two solid days, we worked on connection practices, such as how to first create real connection in communication before seeking agreement or even intellectual understanding on long-standing contentious issues.

We explored healthy boundaries, because boundaries create safety, and safety between two people – not just physical, but mental and emotional safety, too – is absolutely essential for creating a healthy connection. If you don't feel safe with your partner, you can't let your guard down and be authentically vulnerable, which means authentic connection isn't possible.

As the weekend wore on, Stan and Sonya experienced how simple connection practices can literally compel their bodies to come closer together on the couch, and how acting blindly out old patterns of behaviors that create disconnection would immediately send them flying to opposite ends of the room.

It's simple, really. But not easy. For it often requires breaking decades-old unskillful patterns and shifting entrenched limiting beliefs to more open-hearted ways of thinking, seeing, and being. But this is why I love working with couples (and particularly weekend intensives, where we can really practice embodiment).

Intimate relationships are the transformational fires within which all our old wounds and fear-based beliefs will surface so they may finally be witnessed and healed. Fortunately, we don't necessarily need years of therapy to create exquisite moments of connection with each other. After all, we just want to be happy in the moment, with a harmonious, peaceful relationship that lights up our every day life rather than darkens it.

That's what becomes possible when you learn how to create connection first. In fact, you can get through anything together that may arise on this wild human journey when you know how to quickly create connection with your partner. Truly ... *anything.*

I've personally worked with some of the most painfully strained, broken down couples who became long-term success stories because they learned how to overcome their own "crisis of connection."

As for Stan and Sonya, their journey continues since we wrapped up our weekend. I can't know for sure whether they'll stay together. After all, years of painful momentum have brought them to this crisis point.

But this I know with certainty: Creating profound connection requires only the willingness – and the courage – to never stop exploring your partner's authentic heart.

 40

THE SINGLE MOST DESTRUCTIVE CAUSE OF RELATIONSHIP STRESS: RESISTING FEELINGS

For years I couldn't feel my feelings, and my intimate relationships suffered awfully as a result.

I was unable to cry, but I couldn't really laugh, either, certainly not that delicious kind of full-body, life-embracing laughter that erupts from deep inside the belly. With such restricted access to my own feelings, I could never really understanding what my partners were feeling, or why. So I often judged them for feeling at all, which never helped any woman feel safe with me.

I've since come to understand that, for a man to do love well, he must learn to do what for ages our forefathers (and many a foremother) strongly rejected doing: We must learn to FEEL. Everything.

I recently watched the movie "1917", an epic World War 1 tale of two teenage boys sent across enemy lines on a rescue mission to save 1600 men from certain slaughter. As I nibbled bits of dark chocolate while nestled safe in the plush leather recliner of a Hollywood movie theater, I watched these boys on their mission, bravely navigating across a perilous front-line battleground – that death-scarred "no man's land" so often used in movies to represent how many men experience life and relationships, in general.

After narrowly surviving a few awful, tragic events, they cross paths with an elder, ostensibly wiser man. This man, upon catching a glimpse of their upset feelings, calmly yet forcefully urges them to *"move quickly past it, and not dwell on it."*

This theme is repeated throughout the film, as men face the horror and devastation wrought by their own collective madness. We witness a parade of male faces tightening, male eyes hardening, and male jaws locking – the visible evidence of an inner battle against feelings waged and won instantly by the tyrant stoicism we've been sold as "manly."

War isn't the primary tragedy; it's the inevitable consequence of a daily tragedy we needlessly inflict upon ourselves (and others) by clenching tightly down around feelings.

Imagine if men could simply sit and BE with our inner pain, our anger, sadnesses, frustrations, and our grieving, instead of constantly acting out from within it all in desperate and endlessly futile attempts to make it go quickly away?

Instead, we live inside this suffocating choke that hold robs us all of the experience of feeling fully alive, acting out daily in unacknowledged pain. Thus we hurt ourselves and others – causing war – despite our often great intentions.

As both a man who failed at relationship for years, and a relationship coach since, who's seen thousands of people up close struggling with their own, I believe the single most destructive cause of relationship stress is our resistance to simply feeling what is there to be felt.

The single most destructive cause of relationship stress is our resistance to simply feeling what is there to be felt, inside and around us.

It's not money, sex, social media, kids, alcohol, porn, etcetera. Those are but surface ripples radiating out from a core "mission mindset" endlessly hell-bent on getting free of unwanted feelings. How ironic that endless relationship stress is caused by trying to feel no stress at all.

Even knowing this, I still sometimes find myself unconsciously working to argue my lady (or myself) out of whatever she's feeling in the moment, hoping with great futility that if I can simply convince her to feel differently, I will fulfill on my primary mission: Peace and harmony for all. Of course only the opposite ever happens. Because the moment I resist feelings, hers or mine, I start a war – with reality.

A PRACTICE

If you want to shift disharmonious dynamics in your relationship(s) to create more genuine connection, stop arguing over who did what, said what, or wants what. Instead, focus on whatever feelings are arising in the moment, for you and for them.

Practice feeling what is there to be felt, and making it safe for your partner to do the same.

Are you feeling frustrated? Angry? Afraid? Unseen? Hurt? Deflated? Sad? Acknowledge it without trying to attach a reason why, even if you think you know (you almost surely don't).

When two people stop arguing over facts and start focusing on (and sharing in) the *feeling* experiences arising in the moment, however awkward or uncomfortable, connection often begins to happen effortlessly. This is true vulnerability. When we stop attacking each other with our judgments and conclusions, and instead start telling the raw truth about what we're actually experiencing in this moment, we create an opening for the other to be curious, and to care, about us.

If they're worthy of your presence, they'll be willing to meet you there, even if it's uncomfortable.

This is how relationships thrive: Two people daily drawn towards each other through curiosity and caring, rather than repelled by each other because neither feels safe to simply feel what is actually there to be felt.

 41

WHY A MAN CAN LEAVE MANY TIMES (A WOMAN ONLY LEAVES ONCE)

I've seen it countless times: A man can leave a relationship and return, over and over, where a woman can only leave once.

Not only have I seen it as a relationship coach since 2013, I've been that man. In my 30s, throughout the 5 years of an inflamed relationship that profoundly challenged me, I would leave whenever I felt too constricted, too incapable of "solving the problems" the relationship (and this wild, untamable woman whom I wouldn't ever want "tamed" anyway) seemed to be creating for me.

Whether for a few days, or a few weeks, and sometimes a few months, I probably left and came back 20 times – maybe 1000. Sometimes I only left for a few hours, by checking out emotionally. Exhausted from all the fighting (mostly happening in my own brain), my body was present but I was numb to my feelings – and she felt it.

She, on the other hand, never left. Sure, she was angry plenty. But she never left. Actually, instead of leaving she'd straight up confront me, in countless ways demanding, fighting, imploring, manipulating, and at times damn-near torturing me to stay.

It was a bizarre and hurtful dance we did. The more she demanded I show up – for the relationship, for love, for her – the more I desired to leave, even though I didn't really want to leave. Still, whenever things got even a little difficult, by which I mean uncomfortable emotions ran high, she would feel my lack of deep resolve to stay, which only further triggered her demanding that I show up.

It was a nasty cycle, and neither of us knew what was going on … or how to stop it. Thus we spiraled ever downward into the painful depths of relationship hell.

Today I understand why she worked so hard to keep me around, why I ached so strongly to get away, why I always came back, and why she always let me: I was marching to the masculine chant of freedom, and she was dancing to the feminine song of connection.

(Note: there are surely more layers to this, including attachment styles, childhood wounding, trauma bonding, survival beliefs, and more, but I speak here to the primal dance of masculine-feminine intimacy)

Every time I left, I was (unknowingly) leaving to give myself a taste, though fleeting and superficial it surely was, of the freedom I desperately craved to know in my being. Yet after a brief time of superficially blissful separation, I'd feel the irresistible forces of attraction drawing me back to her; feel the longing in my heart to know love; decide I could do things better this time, given the benefit of some newfound clarity I'd discovered in our time apart; and so dive back in! Only to see our sabotaging patterns quickly reassert themselves – often within just days.

For her, it was quite different. While I can't truly know her actual experience, what I personally do know about "the Feminine experience" of intimacy reveals this:

Every time I left, abruptly and dismissively, was yet another axe blow to the roots of connection that bound us together at heart, no matter how far apart we were. Those roots – which she kept vigil over despite our chaos – were so thick we'd sometimes find our way back together from opposite sides of the planet, even despite the presence of other lovers (with whom connecting-roots weren't very strong).

However, after so many assaults on the roots of our connection, she was also – as many women do – grieving the loss of our relationship even as it endured. For when it all finally (finally!) ended one January evening many years ago, when separated by an entire continent between us, I again left her by this time simply refusing to answer her phone call.

Unlike times before when she kept calling until I picked up (once clocked at 82 consecutive calls!! Yes, we were ridiculous), this time she didn't call again. She was done. For not even a month later I learned she was beginning a new life with a new man, a man she would later marry.

My grieving was only just beginning. And I would grieve that relationship for many years to come.

On the surface, it indeed looks like "freedom" and "connection" are in irreconcilable opposition to each other – each existing merely to subvert the other. In co-dependent relationships between people who know very little of real love, like me and my ex, that's exactly what happens as one partner fights more for freedom and the other fights more for connection.

One cries, *"Don't abandon me!"* (connection) as the other protests, *"Don't control me!"* (freedom)

This is how even otherwise great relationships are run to ruin.

Today, I'm once again 5 years into intimate relationship. We've certainly had a few moments when superficial notions of freedom suddenly rose up in protest against the suffocating obligations of co-dependent connection, and indeed, the world burned once again.

However, with the benefit of awareness, insight, and simple practices that honor both freedom (masculine) and connection (feminine), the predominant nature of our intimate relationship is one of appreciation and an embrace of our differences.

Laughter is epidemic in our home as we watch our opposing values clash in ways both mundane and absurd, such as how we simply turn off the light before going to sleep (Silvy tends to want it on longer to keep connecting, while I tend to want it off so I can finally be free of the constricting burdens of the day).

Gone, mostly anyway, are the days when I would unconsciously hack at the roots of connection for fear of losing some freedom.

Which is good news, because we've discovered a magic formula you can follow, too. It's a way of dancing in partnership that can help resolve this primal conflict in our everyday lives together:

The more I help her feel connected, the more quickly she can relax and trust in my presence, which then helps us both feel more free. The more she helps me feel free, the more I feel inspired to really show up for the relationship, and for her, which helps us both feel more connected.

Often we must dance the opposite, for I also sometimes need reassurance of her presence (connection), and she also sometimes needs to know I affirm her right to be whomever she chooses to be (freedom).

Regardless, it really is magic, that when we both stand for connection and for freedom, we both feel more connected and free. Thus we dance the spiral upwards into the relational heavens of genuine partnership, real love. It ain't always an easy dance, but it is always an exquisite one.

Because true freedom can only be found in the land of deep connection.

"We are so connected the word 'connected' doesn't even make sense."

– Rumi

42

CHOOSE HER EVERY DAY
(OR LEAVE HER)

I spent 5 years hurting a good woman by staying with her but never fully choosing her.

I did want to be with this one. I really wanted to choose her. She was an exquisite woman, brilliant and funny and sexy and sensual. She could make my whole body laugh with her quick, dark wit and short-circuit my brain with her exotic beauty. Waking up every morning with her snuggled in my arms was my happy place. I loved her wildly.

Unfortunately, as happens with many young couples, our ignorance of how to do love well quickly created stressful challenges in our relationship. Before long, once my early morning blissful reverie gave way to the strained, immature ways of our everyday life together, I would often wonder if there was another woman out there who was easier to love, and who could love me better.

As the months passed and that thought reverberated more and more through my head, I chose her less and less. Every day, for five years, I chose her a little less.

I stayed with her. I just stopped choosing her. We both suffered.

Choosing her would have meant focusing every day on the gifts she was bringing into my life that I could be grateful for: her laughter, beauty, sensuality, playfulness, companionship, and so ... much ... more.

Sadly, I often found it nearly impossible to embrace – or even see – what was so wildly wonderful about her.

I was too focused on the anger, insecurities, demands, and other aspects of her strong personality that grated on me. The more I focused on her worst, the more I saw of it, and the more I mirrored it back to her by offering my own worst behavior. Naturally, this only magnified the strain on our relationship ... which still made me choose her even less.

Thus did our nasty death spiral play itself out over five years.

She fought hard to make me choose her. That's a fool's task.

You can't make someone choose you even when they might love you.

To be fair, she didn't fully choose me, either. The rage-fueled invective she often hurled at me was evidence enough of that.

I realize now, however, that she was often angry because she didn't feel safe with me. She felt me not choosing her every day, in my words and my actions, and she was afraid I would abandon her.

Actually, I did abandon her.

By not fully choosing her every day for five years, by focusing on what bothered me rather than what I adored about her, I deserted her.

Like a precious fragrant flower I brought proudly into my home but then failed to water, I left her alone in countless ways to wither in the dry hot heat of our intimate relationship.

I'll never not choose another woman I love again.

It's torture for everyone.

If you're in relationship, I invite you to ask yourself this question: *"Why am I choosing my partner today?"*

If you can't find a satisfying answer, dig deeper and find one. It could be as simple as noticing that in your deepest heart's truth, *"I just do."*

If you can't find it today, ask yourself again tomorrow. We all have disconnected days.

But if too many days go by and you just can't connect with why you're choosing your partner, and your relationship is rife with stress, let them go. Create the opening for another human being to show up and see them with fresh eyes and a yearning heart that will enthusiastically choose them every day.

Your loved one deserves to be enthusiastically chosen. Every day.

You do, too.

Choose wisely.

PART 3

TRANSCENDING
THE FIRE

 43

INTIMATE RELATIONSHIP CHANGES YOU (IGNORE ALL ADVICE SAYING OTHERWISE)

Whatever the popular love advice of the day says about *"find someone who loves you as you are"* … sure, that's a wise ideal to lean towards, but make no mistake:

You don't get to stay the same person when you finally decide to build a life with another human being.

Where a "bad" relationship will change you into someone you don't like, and a relationship that doesn't serve to change you at all will eventually bore you, a truly "good" relationship commands you to grow. By good I just mean a relationship that compels you towards becoming the loving, heart-centered, wise being you were born to become. Naturally, all the parts of you that are not yet loving, heart-centered, and wise will resist that push towards growth. (what else could those parts possibly do?)

From the outside looking in, you'd hardly believe both Silvy and I have thought of fleeing our relationship more than a few times in our 3 years together. If not to save our selves from the other, then to save the other from our selves. But Silvy and I met as two individuals deeply committed to growing in love. This relationship of ours continues to command us both to grow in ways we could not choose – would no choose! – to grow by ourselves alone.

That's what makes our relationship great. It's not great because it's easy, or we just somehow get each other. Hell no! We're two passionate, strong-willed people born with meaningfully different biologies who then marinated (for decades) in vastly different life experiences. Our two still-distinct worlds clash often enough!

Our relationship is great because we're both willing to be changed and evolved by this experience in ways that require us to drop our stubborn allegiances to what we each think "should be" and instead learn to more fully embrace "what is wanting to become" ... even when it's uncomfortable.

In other words, our relationship serves to open us both ever more towards Real Love, the mysterious domain of the heart, not of the brain.

I don't care what the latest 27-yr old dating "guru" on YouTube says, Real Love is fucking terrifying to the ego-mind that thinks it knows what love should look like.

Today, I am not the same man Silvy met 3 years ago. For although she does her best to love me "as I am," she also loves me (and herself) in such committed, penetrating ways that the best, most loving man in me is routinely commanded forth because nothing less will serve. I still sometimes (often) resist that command, though in the end it's always futile. For it's my heart, and not merely another ego, always commanding me to grow.

As my resistance relaxes, I allow myself to not know what life should look like right now. This allows my heart to open to what is actually present in the moment, even though my mind may label it ugly and unwanted. In that openness, I can (finally) show up for Love – not just for Silvy, but for

Love – in ways the old Bryan would never have believed possible, would have scoffed at even.

Yet my daily reward for my commitment to growing in love is a brilliant Khoucasian-smile bursting with kindness and affection, and two gorgeous ocean-black Isis eyes in which I get to see reflected back at me all the joys and sorrows and passionate longings of the Universe.

That's the true Alchemy of Love:

When we experience, even for an instant, our humanity transformed to reveal the divine within us, and we suddenly find ourselves in awe, touching the dazzling face of infinity.

Such a blissful freedom as this actually can be found in relationship, but only if you're willing to be forever changed by it.

 # 44

LEARN TO FEEL YOUR WOMAN (OR LOSE HER)

A man recently told me that his wife said she doesn't feel connected to him.

When she said it, he looked around, quickly noticed they were both physically in the same room talking to each other, and exclaimed with frustration drenching his words, *"What the f**k are you talking about? I'm right here!"*

She didn't feel connected to him. When he couldn't make sense of that and angrily said so, she felt even more disconnected. Over time, their relationship crisis would worsen.

Have you experienced this?

Since my viral essay, Choose Her Everyday (Or Leave Her), a lot of women have written me with this complaint about their male partners: *"He doesn't know how to show up."*

These women typically describe how angry, hurt, and frustrated they are that their partners seem to be emotionally and/or psychologically absent from the relationship. Many are about to give up and leave. Some already have. There are also those who stay, and stay miserable.

What are these women pointing to in their pain of disconnection?

It's called Masculine Checkout Syndrome, or MCS (a real condition I made up). In most heterosexual relationships it tends to look like this:

Man is physically present but emotionally and/or psychologically distant. He might say he cares about the relationship and his partner, though he engages more consistently and perhaps more enthusiastically with other aspects of life – work, TV, hobbies, friends, sports, addictions – than he does with her. When he does engage with her, he often does so with indifferent or agitated energy. She feels it; he doesn't … or he pretends not to.

One woman who wrote described her male partner as a good man who usually does the right thing in their relationship. She's deeply dissatisfied by his lack of emotional display. He's physically present, but all she feels is the actual solidity of his body. Sex is dissatisfying because he doesn't use his body to dance in delicious sensual partnership with hers; he's mostly just masturbating himself inside her.

She feels abandoned, even though he physically shows up. Viscerally, she feels unable to trust him.

Here's the essential problem:

He's been taught his entire life – as most men have – to deny his emotions, to deny the body in favor of mental fortitude. As a boy, he was fiercely taught, *"Don't act like a girl!"* and *"Don't be a wussy!"* and *"No pain no gain!"* and *"Stop crying!"* and countless other body-shaming programs.

He was shamed when he let down his veil of invincibility, usually by other men and sometimes by women, too. For women were also taught that vulnerability is akin to weakness, that emotions are inconvenient and burdensome, and that it's best not to express yourself too much lest you annoy others.

When emotions begin to overwhelm – as they often do in the inherently emotional world of intimate relationship, whether erupting from a partner or ourselves – we cut the body cord and retreat into the intellect for safety. Or we eventually express those emotions as anger because that's the emotion of strength, so we've been led to believe. Though many men can't access anger, either, so wary are we of this emotion we've only ever seen used to damage and destroy.

When we can't solve the emotional burdens of the relationship *(Why is she feeling disconnected and upset when I'm right here?)* and anger fails us, we'll turn to solving easier problems at work or in sports, or just watch others do it on TV. Whatever we do, we start separating ourselves from the relationship for mental relief.

Thus, Masculine Checkout Syndrome:

We stop showing up, even if we stay in the room.

A PRACTICE

What to do?

To start: Breathe.

To stay embodied in the presence of an intimate partner who's expressing upset, a simple technique I offer men in my coaching practice – and women, too, for women also embody masculine energy and are susceptible to MCS – is to visualize breathing into your heart.

Breathe consciously, deeply, intentionally, into your own heart. As you exhale, breathe into her heart. She doesn't even have to know you're doing it.

Feel her. Feel into what's really beneath her upset. The woman before you may be masquerading as an exploding nuclear bomb, but she's not an actual bomb. She's simply a woman in pain. She misses you. She misses you in your heart.

Work to cultivate the capacity to stand in front of your partner and just breathe with her. Soften your face, and pour your love into her; breathe into your heart and vision her being filled with your love through your breath. You're not trying to solve her, fix her, shrink her, quiet her, calm her down, have her make any kind of sense to you (or herself), not trying to do anything to or for her other than fill her up with your love.

If we're ever to experience intimate relationship with any sort of deep and abiding fulfillment, this is what's required of us: To come Home to Heart.

We all started out there as little boys, able to cry as easily as we could laugh. Unafraid to cuddle our mothers and embrace our fathers, we offered our emotional feedback to the world without shame. Somewhere along the way we began to bottle it all up, distrusting, even fearing emotions.

I'm not suggesting we return to childish ways of unleashing emotional havoc on the world around us.

I am suggesting that the time has come to temper the rational intelligence of the intellect with the mysterious wisdom of the emotional body. The intellect, though it can serve us well, can also make people do all kinds of things that hurt themselves or others when just one intense thought takes over.

Emotions can offer profound guidance when the intellect fails to comprehend the complexities of any situation. A deeply nourishing emotion can illuminate what's working well in this moment, while a painful one may indicate that something clearly isn't, no matter what the calculating intellect says.

Through their upset, our intimate partners are pointing the way home. They're inviting the masculine force in us all to return triumphantly to our full bodied authentic selves, integrating intellectual intelligence with embodied emotional wisdom.

Your partner's upset is always an invitation for you to come home to your own heart. Breath into your heart. Then breath into hers. It's a start, and it won't solve everything. But when she smiles because she feels you like she hasn't felt you in a long time, you'll know it's a good start.

 45

MEN, SHE NEEDS TO FEEL YOU SAFE (TO TRUST YOU)

Man, whether or not you think she has good reason to distrust you, nature didn't evolve a woman to believe your words, or even your recent past behavior.

Nature evolved her to believe your present state.

She's constantly *feeling you* … right now.

She's also constantly telling you in countless ways either:

> *1. I feel safe with you right now, or*

> *2. I don't feel safe with you right now*

No matter what smart words you're speaking or what thoughtful thing you did even 5 minutes ago, if you don't feel safe to her right now, she won't trust you, nor should she. You don't have to feel good in yourself (happy, joyful, excited, etc.), but you do have to feel safe to her.

She needs to feel you safe so she can trust you. If she doesn't trust you, she can't relax. If she can't relax, she can't open to you. Not authentically, anyway. She might pretend to open to you, emotionally or physically, but she'll only be abusing herself by doing so, which serves no one.

If she can't open to you authentically she can't genuinely give herself to you, emotionally, mentally, or physically. Which only causes frustration, *yours and hers*. Because she's aching to open to you. But she won't if she doesn't feel you safe. Nor should she.

To be clear, feeling safe doesn't mean you should feel castrated, or afraid to show up fully in your passion, your desire. You disconnected from your desire just makes her feel lonely with you, and even more unsafe. Because you disconnected from your desire, your power, signals to her that she still has to protect herself.

Protect herself from what? From this dangerous world that often refuses to acknowledge her needs and feelings matter. Your disconnected self sure can't show up to help her powerfully navigate that unendingly painful experience. She'll also just somehow know she must protect herself from your disconnected self, too: That dark shadow within you that she knows can hurt both of you, whether actively or passively, so long as you refuse to courageously (re)claim it.

Always remember this: As you reject your own desires you will reject her desires, too. As you reject your own feelings, you will reject her feelings, too.

Perhaps the most profoundly empowering work a man can ever do is learn to stay connected to your deepest desires and own your immense inner power, which includes overcoming and integrating anything inside you holding you down in shame. When you learn to face and embrace your inner world, the beautiful and the ugly, you simultaneously discover how to offer all of yourself to her (and to the world) through your enlivened presence, and through gifts of insight and courage, and in ways that she viscerally understands you will never force her (or the world) to do anything against her genuine will.

Thus you become a harbor in which she can always return to feel safe.

A PRACTICE

Start asking yourself:

1. *"Is she communicating now that she feels safe or doesn't feel safe?"*

2. *"How might I show up in this moment – what gift can I offer – that might help her feel more safe?"*

Would it serve to gently touch her arm, or pull her physically closer to you? Would reassuring words help? Could you soften your tone of voice? Perhaps she is sensing that you're stuck in your thoughts and not listening to her, or that you're focusing more on something else in the room (e.g. the TV, or your phone)?

Simply watch what happens in her body when you simply begin this dialogue with yourself. Stay in it until you notice signs of her visibly relaxing – perhaps through a deep breath or her voice softens.

We men must learn to stop leaning on our words or even our past actions as the primary evidence we insist she accept of our trustworthiness and sincerity. Yes all that matters, but far less so than the depth of your presence in the moment.

Learn instead to shift your focus to what you're feeling in your body. I know that's difficult for many men (many women, too), so keep it simple: If you're feeling constriction, tension, fear, worry, anger, disgust, etc. anywhere in your body, she's almost certainly feeling it, too, in both you and in herself.

Practice focusing on your own feelings first. Stop trying first to get her (or your bank account, boss, kid, traffic, republicans, democrats, etc.) to change so you can feel better. It won't work, anyway, not for long. Something else will always arise to frustrate you. So learn to

change your own physical state first, regardless of what is happening outside you.

You can always take a break from the interaction. Go for a walk. Watch a sunset. Eat something yummy and nourishing. Take a shower. Or just breathe. Shift your breathing, from short and shallow, to patient and deep. One of my favorite breathing practices is consciously *allowing* my breath to be a little deeper with each breath, *without forcing it to be deeper.*

Any of these simple actions can help you settle your own nervous system, which can make you feel safer inside yourself. Which in turn can help her feel safer, too. You can only do your part; she surely has her own (inner) work to do, too.

Just don't fool yourself into thinking you've done all you can:

In my experience, personal and professional, I'd say about 100% of the time we men have yet more to learn, and therefore more to offer, that would make a meaningful difference in helping our intimate partner feel consistently more safe in our presence.

 ## 46

TIRED OF YOUR PARTNER NOT 'ENTHUSIASTICALLY CHOOSING' YOU?

Are you fed up with NOT being enthusiastically chosen every day in your intimate relationship?

Since *"Choose Her Every Day (or Leave Her)"* went viral, I've heard from countless disheartened women and men all over the world about their painful experiences with intimate partners who aren't very enthusiastic around doing relationship with them. I was surprised to discover that this is a tragically common experience, and that many people can stay in such deeply dissatisfying relationships for years, even *decades*.

I've been asked over and over:

"How do you get a partner to show up when they seem to prefer work, TV, porn, friends, internet, fantasy football, or even just silence instead of you?"

Below I offer 3 empowering practices to ensure you're never not chosen again.

I caution you: This will require profound courage on your part.

Why? Because you must fully take responsibility for your own well-being. You must learn the confronting practice of not believing your bullshit ways of thinking that have you saddling others with the ill-fitting burden of your happiness and contentment. Anyway, your partner (or future partner) probably struggles at least to some degree to consistently manage their own well-being; yet you expect them to manage yours, too?

Even many strong, independent people cling stubbornly to the fantasy that a partner will somehow complete you. No matter your intelligence, you may still persist in your longing for some white knight or wild divine goddess partner who comes bearing all the riches and tasty rewards your ravenously insatiable soul yearns for!

Or maybe your endless disappointments caused you to kill and bury that white knight goddess dream long ago. Perhaps you can barely bring yourself to wish for even a small kindness anymore from your partner – a kind word, a warm embrace, or just a loving glance during commercials.

Here's what you must know:

Your partner will never give enthusiastically what you selfishly demand of them.

For example, when a woman *demands* a man's presence – by insisting he go out less with his friends or spend more time with her on Saturdays – that man might yield, but resentment will build inside him like heart-clogging plaque. In the same way, a woman's resentment can only deepen and her heart close a little more each time she says yes to an emotionally disconnected man who's using her body for his shallow pleasure.

However, when you learn to see beyond the popular delusion that your happiness depends on a partner, you actually start attracting the damn-sexy-best out of anyone who's deeply ready to offer it.

If your current partner isn't ready (or willing) to offer you their damn-sexy-best, at least now you've the inner strength to walk away and ready yourself for someone who is. A curious side-effect can happen when you stop choosing someone who has stopped enthusiastically choosing you: *They may rediscover their enthusiasm for you.*

Here's 3 ways to ensure you're *never not chosen* again:

1. Always Give Feedback, Never Criticism.

Feedback is about your experience, what you are feeling, seeing, thinking. Feedback lets the other person know what you're going through in their presence. Feedback doesn't make your upsets their fault.

Criticism, on the other hand, makes your upset your partner's fault. Criticism is your personal opinion about what your partner should be doing or saying, which is actually not your business. Whether you've just started dating or been married for 20 years with 12 kids together, your partner is their own unique person on their own personal journey through life.

When you tell him (or her) what you think they are doing wrong, how they can do it better or that they can't do it right at all, you turn yourself into the boss they don't want ... or worse, the parent they resent.

If your partner is more masculine (or you want them to be), your criticism offends their core masculine value: Freedom.

Criticism screams, *"You are not free to do as you please! You should do it like I say you should."*

Your partner will almost surely first react by defending against your criticism before they can hear what you're really saying. If you can first respect their right to choose and live as they wish, you'll help them feel respected and honored. This can help them better hear you, too.

This does not mean you should hang around while your partner is doing or saying something hurtful or that you really don't enjoy being around.

No. This is where feedback is absolutely essential. Telling your partner how their behavior, their words, affect you is the only way someone truly willing to learn how to love you can actually learn how to love you. The same words and actions don't touch everyone the same. A word or action that hurts you might not hurt someone else.

But how can your partner know you're hurting unless you tell them?

By giving feedback without the criticism you honor the partnership; your relationship no longer becomes an adversarial battle. Your partner can relax their inner freedom-fighter and instead focus on how to show up for your concerns. If they routinely dismiss your feedback and show no willingness to grow in love with you, leave.

Why would you stay with a partner who routinely dismisses you, who isn't willing to learn how to love you?

2. Enthusiastically Choose Your Partner.

When you partner with someone, you get all of him (or her). If you want him to change, maybe he's not the right partner for you. He may or may not change as life evolves, but that's not your business.

If you can't fully accept and embrace your partner for all that he is today, why are you with him? Are you afraid to be alone? That's no reason to be in a relationship.

You're better off staying single until you are so comfortable with yourself that only someone who makes your great life even better will do for you.

If you can't fully accept the partner you're with, they won't likely be fully accepting of you, either. They'll feel your ongoing judgment, your lack of acceptance. They'll be too busy managing their own insecurities to love you through yours.

If you want to be fully chosen by your partner, then fully choose your partner. If you can't, leave so someone else can, and get to work on choosing yourself.

3. Enthusiastically Choose Yourself.

Refuse to settle for less than what your deepest heart desires. Stay busy creating the most exquisite, delicious life for yourself you can possibly imagine.

If you're with someone today, your commitment to creating the best life for yourself will inspire them to do the same just to keep up with you! Or it'll send them packing once their lack of commitment to living their best life reveals itself. Either way, you keep moving forward into the life of your dreams.

Sure, every relationship has ups and downs. Cycles are the way of life. Your relationship will have its cycles, its seasons, too.

But if your partner isn't willing to grow and expand their capacity to love, why keep them around? You're just sentencing your relationship to stagnation, if not death.

Anyway, I believe the best we can ever hope for is a partner who's simply willing to keep showing up, who's willing to learn how to do this wild masculine-feminine dance of opposites with at least a little more grace and tenderness and flow and laughter and love than we knew yesterday.

In the end, whether you're single or in relationship, stay focused on creating your best life for yourself. When you're focused on creating amazing every day, you naturally attract others committed to creating amazing every day, too.

It's delicious irony: The best way to ensure your partner enthusiastically chooses you is to LET GO needing a partner to enthusiastically choose you … and focus instead on enthusiastically choosing yourself every day!

47

THE ONE SHIFT IN COMMUNICATION (THAT SAVES RELATIONSHIPS)

"When someone comes to you with their pain,
they're not asking you to decide if their experience is valid."
– Silvy Khoucasian

Through all my adventures in intimacy, I spent way too much time evaluating the validity of my partners' upsets and frustrations – often deciding they are NOT valid, especially when directed at me.

This was essentially my initial response when faced with a woman's upset:

"Look, I have great intentions. If you can't see that, then you need to change how you see things, to end this pointless complaint. Also, outside of convincing you to see things my way, I have no other role to play in helping you feel better."

Somehow, that never went over well – to my great and enduring surprise!

It wasn't until my late 30s (I'm now 46) that I started to understand something profound about how I was (unwittingly) sabotaging intimacy: With great intentions, I was trying to "set my partner free in her mind" by using logic and perspective (my own) so she would see things differently. Yet what she often only wanted was to restore "the feeling of connection with me" in the moment – which has nothing to do with logic (not mine, anyway).

My goodness! What countless epic battles and mighty defeats could we all have avoided had someone simply taught me this fundamental truth of intimate relationship between the two complementary energies of masculine and feminine expression!

Everything changed for me once I started to understand that every intimate relationship, regardless of sexual orientation, is a primal dance between masculine and feminine energies. *(Note: masculine does not mean "man" and feminine does not mean "woman")*

One of the most profound changes was in the actual words I started using to communicate.

The Focus of Your Language: Freedom or Connection

I learned there is a fundamental difference in the *focus of communication* between masculine and feminine energies. Our ignorance of this difference causes endless painful misunderstandings.

A more "core-feminine" person (man or woman) tends to communicate more with CONNECTION-FOCUSED LANGUAGE: words that ask and imply, *"Are we in this together? Because we should (better!) be!"*

A more "core-masculine" person (man or woman) tends to communicate more with FREEDOM-FOCUSED LANGUAGE: words that imply, *"I'll make my own choices, think my own thoughts, and be my own person. You should (better!) do the same."*

Understanding these differences in communication focus taught me how to start defusing difficult moments that may otherwise destroy intimacy and ruin relationships.

For example, for years I (unskillfully) used *freedom-focused language* with my more *connection-focused* partners:

> *"Stop trying to control me; I don't try to control you!"*
> *"Stop making up problems that don't exist!*
>   ["problems" limit freedom]
> *"Don't tell me how I should think!"*
>   [how ironic I often told them how to think]
> *"Don't tell me how to do what I know how to do."*

I was unable to hear their typically (and unskillfully) *connection-focused* responses:

> *"Do you even care about me?"*
> *"Do you really want to be with me?"*
> *"Why don't my feelings matter to you?"* [shared feelings is
>   empathy, connection]
> *"I don't feel connected to you."* [like many men, I heard it
>   but dismissed it as a "made-up" complaint]

I was shocked to discover we were speaking the same language but oriented towards very different core values (connection vs freedom).

Through coaching couples since 2013, I see this misunderstanding constantly, in heterosexual and same-sex relationships. Even in heterosexual relationships, sometimes it's a man who's more connection-focused while his female partner is more focused on expressing her freedom.

How can you know if you (or your partner) are more core-feminine (connection-focused) or core-masculine (freedom-focused)?

Although many people tend to identify with one over the other, some regularly switch back and forth between both. I identify as more core-masculine, as freedom tends to be my primary concern, yet I have a lot of feminine moments when I need more connection-affirming language from my partner. Knowing this, sometimes she'll reassure me during a difficult conversation by saying, *"I'm not going anywhere; we'll get through this together."*

My dad left home when I was 4, and this permanent cleaving of my family caused a deep wound that lives in me as the feminine fear of abandonment. When my partner says *"I'm not going anywhere,"* her words help calm me.

Whether your partner predominantly lives in one or daily flirts between both, you can hear their underlying focus in their language, particularly in moments of stress or upset, or when speaking aspirationally about what they yearn for:

– Do they talk about feeling trapped by circumstances, lack of options or possibilities, or by political or philosophical ideas they don't like? (freedom-focused)

– Do they point at feeling disconnected from themselves or others, uncared for, unloved, or lonely, abandoned by you, by others, by life? (connection-focused)

– Do they dismiss or deny feelings in favor of facts and solutions? (freedom-focused)

– Do they tend to dismiss details or facts as irrelevant, staying more rooted in feelings? (connection-focused)

The point isn't to clearly know whether you're more "feminine" or "masculine." It doesn't actually matter. We are all being called at this time to learn how to integrate BOTH masculine and feminine energies in our own body-minds. For true mastery as a human being is knowing how to express feminine energy (connection-focus) when that serves the moment, and how to offer masculine energy (freedom-focus) when that serves the moment.

What truly matters, when it comes to creating a thriving relationship, is learning that how you respond matters, and that you can respond using the language-focus the other needs to hear. What matters is that you know you do have a role to play in helping your partner feel reassured and calmed whatever their upset.

If you want a thriving intimate relationship, you must learn how to reassure your partner not using the words you want to hear, but the words they need to hear. Otherwise, your partner – and you – will keep spiraling into distress, disharmony, disconnection, potentially for a lifetime.

A PRACTICE

If you're with a more core-feminine person, when they're upset, never say (even with your eyes):

> *"You should see this differently."*
> *"That's your problem, not mine."*
> *"I don't have time for this."*
> *"Why are you telling me this? I'm not your therapist."*
> *"Sucks to be you!"*
> *"Well, what about MY problem/upset/complaint?"*
> *"Don't start that again. It's always the same thing."*

Instead, try:

> *"I'm sorry you're hurting; we'll figure this out together."*
> *"I hear you. I'm with you."*
> *"I'm not able to hear this right now, but I want to hear it; can we find another time to talk about it (within 24 hours)?"*

If you're with a more core-masculine person, if you're feeling dismissed by their loyalty to logic (their own logic), never say (even with your body):

"You don't care about me!"
"You're so insensitive."
"Why can't you listen to me?"
"You're too much in your head."
"Stop making this about you."
"Stop invalidating my experience."
"What you did was wrong."
"You should have done X differently."

Instead, try:

"I know you're doing your best, and I love you for that. I'm confident we'll figure out how to bridge this difference between us."
"I see your good intentions, and I appreciate you for it."
"I didn't like what you did, but you have every right to do whatever you want to do." (Doesn't mean you're gonna keep hanging around if he/she keeps doing things you don't like; and you might tell them that, too)
"I know you see things a certain way, and I respect that. It would help me feel better if you simply try to understand my point of view, my experience, even if you don't agree with it."
"I know it's hard for you to understand me sometimes, and I don't fault you for that."

Sometimes, it may not be your place to help your partner when they're upset, or going through something difficult. After all, you're not their therapist, their coach, or their parent. If you don't think it's your place to help them with their upset, it's ok to say:

"I don't think I'm the right person to hear this, but I want you to know I love you, and I support you in getting through this. Is there another way I can help?"

If they're upset and asking you for something you know can't (or just won't) give, don't even try to resolve things when they (or you) are still upset. Instead, try this:

"I see this is upsetting you. Your upset is valid. I'm not clear right now how I can best help us resolve this (what you're asking for doesn't register now as the best solution for us both), so let's talk about this later when we're both feeling less triggered."

If this is deeply triggering for one or both of you, I suggest saying this:

"Let's not try to figure this out by ourselves. It's too charged for us, and I don't want us to do more damage to the relationship. Let's bring this to a therapist / coach, who can help us see more clearly what's really going on, and how we can get through this together."

I know this is easier to read here than to actually say when it matters most. This often isn't easy for me, either, and I still regularly fail to say the words most helpful to my partner. But I'm able to catch myself quickly, usually within minutes, and so help us recover quickly before a nasty death-spiral kicks in.

You can learn this, too. Fortunately it only requires practice, patience – with yourself, especially – and real commitment to deep, loving partnership with your beloved.

 48

WITHOUT A SHARED PURPOSE (YOUR RELATIONSHIP WILL FAIL)

For nearly 3 decades, choosing me as your boyfriend was like strapping yourself into a faulty emotional roller coaster whose wheels would scream and spark before jumping the tracks, offing us both towards an awful demise.

Sure, there was always that initial promising climb towards a giddy peak of excitement. But what always inevitably followed was a screaming plunge into undulating whip-lash twists and turns of confusion, chaos, and anger, capped off by a final plummet into heart-crushing disappointment.

What I'm saying is I never made for a very good boyfriend (or husband). Though I never knew why, or even began taking any responsibility, until my late 30s.

I'm engaged now, five years into the relationship I always dreamed possible. The one that keeps proving that old adage: *"When you finally find the right person, it finally makes sense why all those before never worked out."*

Though there's surely truth to that, perhaps it's equally true – and maybe more true – that I finally *became* the right person: A man who could actually pull this relationship thing off.

Silvy is a brilliant, sexy, beautiful, talented, scrumptiously divine woman. Any man would be a right fool to let her go. She is also a reflection of the

Man I have had to become (and am still becoming) if I was ever going to make relationship with such a woman – or any woman – truly thrive, rather than merely keep driving love off the rails into excruciating oblivion.

I only know this because about 18 months into our relationship, I hit a wall.

Even though we had a beautiful connection and so, so many more things were right about our relationship than wrong with it, we had nonetheless been clashing over a cultural divide that even one of the most brilliant therapists in the world told us in a private session is unlikely to ever go away. After a little over a year together, that clash seemed to hit cataclysm status, and I found myself in painfully familiar territory. I feared this roller coaster was about to jump the tracks again.

I was sure I didn't want to lose this extraordinary woman I'd waited a lifetime for, so I hired my own life coach, a man I knew would understand both my culture and my dilemma, a man I could therefore trust to help me navigate this scary situation with more clarity and intention.

In our first session, he asked me a question that caused a seismic shift in my experiencing of relationship:

"Bryan, what is the purpose of your relationship? Is it to have kids? Or build wealth? Or worship God? … What is your purpose for this relationship?"

I already knew the answer. I just hadn't considered the implications of it until that moment.

The core purpose for our relationship is to grow in our capacity to Love.

Many years ago I lived with a woman I wanted to love who did not value "growing" like I did. She seemed to mostly just want an honest man, a cozy home, and healthy kids. She didn't have sincere interest in personal growth workshops, books, retreats, or any such inner/outer adventures – all the things I was a total junkie for.

There's nothing wrong with what she wanted. I'm excited to be creating that homey kinda life with Silvy today. It's also fine she didn't value personal growth. Countless couples endure a lifetime together without growth as a core aspect of their shared purpose.

Nonetheless, because our purposes for the relationship were at painful odds, we kept trying to pull each other in directions the other did not (yet) want to go. The brakes on our bumpy ride heated up as resentments grew and festered. Before long, those brakes went out completely as our grinding attempts to move forward caused us to lose respect for each other, which is when things turned catastrophic for us.

Some version of this played out in most every relationship throughout my 20s and 30s, though I mostly only thought I hadn't yet found the right woman. The reality is I had no meaningful context – or purpose – for why I was ever in relationship at all, other than, *"I simply want fulfilling and drama-free companionship with a woman on my terms."*

Which, I have found, is the perfect purpose if you want to completely fail at relationship.

All relationships will face difficult times. Every couple will experience some hardship together, some gap in understanding, worldview, core values, cultural practice, or some significant external event, perhaps the loss of a loved one, or work, or an addiction – something that will push you both to the edge of your capacity to stay connected. If you don't have a shared purpose for being together, there are endless pressures that can completely derail your intimacy together, even if you physically stay together.

A shared purpose can keep your wheels on the track through even the most difficult times together.

Silvy and I are deeply bound by our mutual commitment to growing in love together. We're excited to have kid(s?) and all that white-picket-fence stuff.

But it's our commitment to growth that binds us at our core. We both experience our relationship as a beautiful container for the ongoing expansion of our minds, the healing of old internal wounds, and our growing capacity to live authentic and powerful as heart-connected, loving human beings. Our commitment to growth extends to our work, too, where Silvy serves other people's desire to grow through her work as a Marriage and Family Therapist, and I serve others as a writer, public speaker, Life Coach and Relationship Coach.

Our choice to stay together wouldn't be right for everyone. Certainly not if your purpose for relationship is having an easy, quiet home life and kids; or economic stability; or merely a companion or lover; or mom's approval, or dad's, or God's; or a green card; or whatever else one might hold consciously or otherwise as their purpose for relationship.

Sometimes Silvy and I *wish* our only purpose was an easy home life, or a green card! For a commitment to growth ain't for the timid of heart! Although it does make for the most thrilling roller coaster ride I've ever been on, and that also just continues to get better, more deeply enriching and satisfying as we go.

So, if you're in a relationship, ask yourself, *"What is the purpose of my relationship?"*

If you're single, ask yourself, *"Why do I want to be in one?"* (you can admit it: you totally do.)

It's ok if your purpose changes over time.

Whatever your purpose for relationship is today, it can be profoundly empowering to know it for yourself, and communicate it with clarity and kindness to whomever you're dancing with now, or in the future. Otherwise, you might be strapping into a roller coaster neither of you wants to ride.

 49

BEATING JEALOUSY:
TWO SIMPLE TRUTHS

Jealousy.

That scourge of intimacy that, at its worst, can rob even the most sane person of his or her mental stability as it drags them disoriented and damned into a fiery living nightmare where they're likely to be tortured by their own fantastical fictions.

When jealousy settles into a relationship the consequences can be severe, even fatal.

It happened to me a few years back. Jealousy ate me and a past love alive from the inside out like Ebola. Relentless and ferocious, it took five years to eviscerate our relationship of every beautiful possibility it began with. When it finally finished us off, jealousy had left us with little but rage, resentment and regret that took years to heal.

Jealousy essentially boils down to this: "I'm horrified you're not going to choose me."

It gets really bad when that horror grabs our innards and makes us act in awful ways that drive the person of our yearning even farther away – if not physically, then emotionally and psychologically. After all, who in their right mind happily chooses to be with a crazy person?

That's what jealousy can do: make us act insane.

An ex-girlfriend once wrecked her car while driving all fast and furious to disrupt a lunch I told her I was having with a woman she didn't want me lunching with. I knew this woman was no threat to our relationship; I wasn't nearly as attracted to her as I was to my girlfriend. But my girlfriend was caught up in the fear-fueled fantasy that I was choosing this other woman instead of her.

You can't make someone choose you. Why would you want to, anyway? Actually, here's why:

When we believe that another person's love, affection, attention or validation is the source of our sense of self-worth or identity, we'll do almost anything to make them stay. We'll use fear, guilt, coercion, even shame and force to keep them around.

Ironically, the consequences of such adversarial actions usually keep away the very things we ache for: connection, trust, appreciation, fulfillment, joy, love.

Have you ever really felt appreciative and loving towards someone who used fear or force to make you do what they wanted? I haven't. I might have done the thing they wanted, but I secretly resented them for it. Or I resented myself for choosing to live out their desires at the precious cost of my own.

There are two powerful truths that can help us beat jealousy and create thriving intimate relationships:

1. Your partner will either choose you everyday or they won't.

There's nothing wrong with not choosing the partner you're with today. It happens all the time and doesn't even have to mean the end of the relationship. It shows up in lots of ways: prioritizing work or kids over partner, emotionally checking out, cheating, breaking up. Regardless what it looks like, relationships begin to break down when one or both partners stop consistently choosing the other.

In my jealousy-infected relationship, I loved my girlfriend, but in my immaturity and ignorance I too often chose friends, work and other priorities over her, like lunch with another woman I was not even romantically interested in. She then punished me by abusing me verbally and withholding love in countless ways. This only reinforced my ignorance-fueled drive to choose others more, which only fueled her anger more. That nasty cycle drove us deep into that years-long living nightmare I described above.

A thriving, sustainable intimate relationship is one in which two people consciously and consistently choose each other over other possibilities, day after day – and in which they both work to communicate that ongoing choice to each other in tangible ways everyday.

I believe we all yearn not merely to be with someone, but to be with someone that we enthusiastically choose everyday, and who enthusiastically chooses us everyday, too. Why would we want to experience anything less than that?

2. Your partner is not the source of your self-worth or self-respect.

It used to be devastating when a woman I wanted didn't choose me. It would trigger old and excruciating wounds of unworthiness and disconnection. A woman's rejection just confirmed what I feared most about myself: I'm not good enough or worthy of love. I've discovered that's an awful lie I've been living inside for a long time – that so many of us live inside.

As a progeny of Life itself, I am an absolute miracle in this very moment, no matter what I look like, how much money I have, whether my grammar is perfect or my socks match. Whether a woman chooses me or not, the fact that I am Earth itself, come alive, walking around with a brain and a heart and the ability to string words into sentences, makes me entirely worthy of love and admiration.

You too, are a wondrous miracle of Earth come alive, the end product in this moment after billions of years of stars exploding and reforming, primordial stuff being ripped apart and then fused back together in infinite experimental forms since the beginning of time.

We completely forget how miraculous we are to simply be thinking, breathing, doing, speaking, loving creatures alive. It's both unnecessary and inappropriate to make other two-legged earth-bodies the arbiters of our inherent value and self-worth when they're just as ignorant as anyone about what we're actually doing here wandering about this lonely planet.

When I really get that my partner isn't the source of my self-worth I can let her choose whatever she wants for herself. She's free to be her and I'm free to be me.

Beating jealousy really comes down to making peace with this simple truth: She is either going to choose me or she isn't.

Whether she chooses me or not, that says nothing about who I actually am. If I try to make her choose what isn't deeply true for her, she'll just resent me for it. Curiously, though, I've found this opens up an exciting possibility.

When we allow our partners the sincere freedom to choose as they desire – even to the extent that we make peace with the possibility that they may actually not choose us – we often become even more attractive to them.

For the one thing most people so deeply want in an intimate relationship is to be with a partner who not just accepts them for who they truly are, but who enthusiastically chooses them for it. If your partner doesn't enthusiastically choose you, let them go. You want a partner, not a prisoner.

If your partner chooses another, allowing them the freedom to do so and letting them go if that's not ok with you simply means you're sparing yourself from someone who isn't choosing you. Maybe they just don't know how. I didn't know how to really choose a woman until I recently hit 40 and finally saw the innocence in my ignorance.

I know it isn't easy, and it might sting, a lot sometimes. But in letting someone go who isn't enthusiastically choosing you, you make room for someone who will. That's so worth waiting for.

 50

THE THIRD TRUTH
TO BEAT JEALOUSY

Recently I started dating an incredible woman who attracts men to her like bees to a sunlit sunflower.

She is an absolute light in this world, radiant from the inside and gorgeous all over the outside. She's kind to strangers and shares her sunshine smile freely. I'd be dumb as a lap dog if I didn't think attraction was happening in her presence everyday. Men are drawn to her constantly. I also know there are times when she's attracted right back.

Attraction just happens. It's like tripping over a rock. Masculine energy is drawn towards feminine energy, and vice versa. It's everyday physics, and it happens all the time.

Yes, I do get jealous. I hadn't really noticed until I started dating this exotically beautiful woman that men are everywhere! I routinely hear her innocently recount interactions with other men. No matter how insignificant the story – like the TSA security guy at the airport who made her laugh during their 15-second encounter – that familiar angst quickly seeps into my gut and quietly whispers, *"he wants to take her away from you."*

All this inspired my recent article, "Beating Jealousy: Two Simple Truths," in which I wrote the two truths are:

1. She's either going to choose me or she isn't.

2. She isn't the source of my self-worth, respect or identity.

There's a third truth I want to add:

3. She is not mine to keep, and she never will be.

I don't own her. No matter what I may ever do "for" her or how long we're together, why would I even try to demand she do anything other than what she deeply believes would be best for her own happiness – even if that means choosing another man?

She's dealt with a lot of insecurity from boyfriends past who would rather shrink her light than face their own sense of insufficiency. I have also experienced the nasty strangling effect of jealousy's poison in my past relationships. One past girlfriend was so racked by fear that I would cheat on her that she hurled invective at me for years, telling me over and over that I was completely unworthy of any other woman. I stayed, in part, because I actually believed her.

I refuse to let that noxious energy infect this new relationship. I love playfully and poetically calling her "my woman," but I refuse to think her radiant brilliance and beauty somehow belong to me. I resist believing that she exists for my pleasure alone.

As soon as I believe I own the gift of her light, I'll want her to dim it down when I'm not around.

Jealousy demands that our partners shrink so we can feel safe in believing no one else will be so drawn to them that they'll try to rob us of our happiness. The irony is that it actually preemptively robs us of that very happiness, in obvious contempt of our desperate attempts to keep it. What's wrong with other people being attracted to our partners? Or our partners being attracted to other people?

I don't want an open-relationship. I don't intend on sleeping with other women, and I don't want my partner to sleep with other men. I'm merely talking about giving her the freedom to share her beauty, her kindness and her light with the world around her. Which means allowing her the freedom to fully interact with men I know will be attracted to her, even sexually attracted.

That's where these three truths to beating jealousy are useful: (1) She's either going to choose me or she isn't. (2) She's not the source of my self-worth. (3) I will never own her, nor should I want to.

I want a partner who chooses me freely, not out of some imagined obligation. What fun would that be for either of us?

I absolutely want a woman that draws men to her. Not for some perverse pleasure (not that there's anything wrong if it were for such pleasure), but because I want a woman in my life who is all lit up, who walks confident through the world connected to her innate wild radiant brilliance. A woman like that is going to attract throngs of fascinated men.

Sure, part of me worries that I will lose her to some other man she suddenly decides is more interesting than I. But I know that grasping desperately at her, insisting that she shrink herself to make me feel better is more likely to create the very scenario I'd be trying to avoid: her choosing another.

Actually, she'd be attracted to that new man because he would only support and encourage her radiance, at least in the beginning, anyway. Until he starts thinking her beautiful light belongs to him alone, and then …

No thanks. I refuse to ask my woman to shrink herself for my peace of mind. I want the freedom to be my best self in the world. So I need to give her the freedom to be her best self in the world, too, even if that means she'll attract lots of men.

In the end, I've realized that the absolute best strategy to attracting and keeping an amazing woman by my side is to simply create an amazing life everyday, independent of whether she chooses me.

Curiously, I notice that as I create an amazing life I love everyday and completely encourage her to shine her light in the world for all to see, she keeps choosing me with her big sunshine smile.

 # 51

HOW TO GET A MAN INTO HIS HEART

No one ever taught me how to *"be in my heart"* ... or what that even means.

My relationships have often suffered horribly as a result.

Like most men (many women, too) I've been conditioned to live in my head, to use my brain to solve any problem that presents itself. And actually, I was taught to see all of life as an unending set of problems to be solved. Eventually, I came to see every woman I loved as a problem to solve, too.

As a young man, I got the message that emotions and feelings are inconvenient, irrational, unnecessarily messy. When I joined the military, the government spent millions to formally train me in what pop-culture sold: Feelings just get in the way of getting shit done.

Thus I was conditioned to not feel what I feel. Thus I learned, like so many men, to keep my heart closed to my own vulnerability, my authentic expression, and by extension, closed to yours, too.

If you're a woman, being in the presence of a man who's heart feels closed can be excruciating! Particularly when you yearn to love and be loved by him, yet all he sees is you as a problem to be solved.

When a man can't connect to heart, he turns so much about a woman into something that needs fixing.

If she's having an upset and insisting it's his fault, he will almost certainly resist and dismiss her. Anything about her that doesn't make logical sense to him, or that he experiences as an obstacle to the outcome he wants, he dismisses, even if only with a mental roll of his eyes. She feels his disconnect from heart, and it hurts her. He also hurts. Deeply. Profoundly. He just can't admit it – or maybe even see it. Still, everyone loses.

I still sometimes grapple with this in my own relationship. When my partner feels me disconnected from my heart, stuck in my logical mind, it can be devastating to her. So when a woman recently asked me, *"How do you get a man into his heart?,"* I searched my own heart for wisdom.

You can't "get a man to do" anything he doesn't genuinely want to do. If you can, you won't respect him, and he won't respect himself, either. But we do need support. Because we cause so much pain to ourselves and others when we can't connect with heart.

So this is for you, if you ache to feel the heart of the man you love. How do you get a man into his heart?

1. You model it for him.

It's a bit disingenuous to expect a man to "be in his heart" if you're not.

If you're stuck in your head, too, where fear, judgment, shame, and blame roost, and you merely projectile vomit that inner turmoil onto him, you're gonna inspire his resistance, not his heart-connect.

Remember, his programming causes him to first evaluate whether your words have logical merit. If he finds fault with your view, he's sure to resist you there.

When you can see your partner having a rough moment as he tries to work out the logic of what's going on (ie. he's stuck in his head), often the least helpful thing you can do is try to convince him he's wrong or that he should just agree with your logic. An even less helpful thing you can do is tell him he's stuck in his head and needs to get into his heart.

Personally, when I'm told I need to think or do something differently – even if my woman is right – what happens is I get hit with a massive surge of inner resistance arising in me like a tsunami. Suddenly, it's even more difficult to connect with my heart, and damn near impossible to connect with hers.

What you can do, which is effective though terrifying, is simply acknowledge the depths of your authentic feelings. When you allow yourself to be vulnerable and honest about your pain, fear, shame, sadness, anger, etc. you keep yourself connected to your own heart. It takes real courage to stay connected to your own feelings and avoid telling him what he needs to do about it.

An ex-girlfriend once told me, *"I'm afraid to be afraid."* Whenever she resisted her fear, she would tear into me like a pitbull tears into a meat-flavored rag-doll. Which she could only do with a closed heart.

When you resist feeling what you're really feeling, you close your own heart.

That's what your man is regularly experiencing. He's terrified to feel what he really feels in his heart, so he buries it beneath thick, icy layers of emotionless mind-manure. If you want your man to connect with his heart, model it by staying connected to yours. Allow yourself to fully feel what you feel, when you feel it.

When my partner fully acknowledges her feelings – especially without judging me or blaming me – the armor around my heart often begins to melt immediately.

2. Don't judge or blame him for what you're feeling.

Yes, a man can be thoughtless, insensitive, and do all kinds of things on a damn near daily basis that seem to prove he has absolutely no regard for your feelings.

Hello! That's how anyone behaves when they're not connected to heart! If he can't feel his own heart, how can he possibly feel yours?

Even a man who can feel will still sometimes speak or act in ways that trigger your upset. That's because it's *your upset*. Which has nothing to do with him, no matter how convinced you are that it does (a juicy topic for another blog).

Whether or not you accept that, whenever you feel threatened, you put up a wall, don't you? Same goes for him.

Men tend to be overly identified with what we do. We derive self-worth from how well we do or fix things. We tend to think it's our job to make you happy, or at least not piss you off. It isn't, but we (mostly) don't know that.

When he senses you negatively judging what he's doing, or he thinks that what he's doing may be hurting you, despite his best intentions, he feels shame. Any man's first instinct will be to run from his shame by closing his heart.

If you can fully feel what you're feeling and not judge or blame him for it, even if his actions did trigger it, you give him at least a fighting chance to soften his resistance, avoid hitting shame, and just be present with you. Yes, absolutely offer your feedback to him about what you're experiencing. Just stay away from criticizing him, even if his actions really are triggering your upset.

Consider: Are you really "in your own heart" when you're criticizing him or telling him he needs to do it different?

It's natural that you want him to feel what you feel. Of course you want his empathy, to feel him "in his heart." That's how you feel most connected to him. But if he's been burying what he feels for a long time, your emotional range will be much wider than his. If he's well practiced at heart-disconnect, then you'll be better at connecting to heart than he is.

It doesn't serve either of you to judge or shame him further for being disconnected, for not feeling what you feel, when it isn't his fault that life taught and conditioned him this way.

3. Hold him accountable.

The worst thing you can ever do for a man is let him get away with loving small. If only because that gives him no incentive to learn, grow, and open up to his own heart.

Modeling it for him and not judging him are a great start, but you can't demonstrate over and over that you're satisfied with a man who's heart is consistently closed and expect him to change.

Make no mistake:

When you stay with him even as he clearly refuses to grow or open, you teach him that he doesn't actually have to grow or open. He learns that you stay, no matter what he does. Why change?

Men grow through challenge. We rise – or sink – to the level of the competition. If he knows you'll let him get away with most anything outside of cheating on or beating you, he will get lazy and stop trying to connect with you. But if he knows you will leave if you don't consistently feel connected to him – and you might even have to actually leave him before he gets that – then if he really wants to be with you, he'll figure it out.

Indeed, a lot of men start coaching with me only *after* they have discovered the hard way that their intimate partner isn't settling for any more hollow assurances.

Sadly, though, I still hear from women every day who've spent years with a man who clearly refuses to grow in love, insisting they've done everything they know to "get him in his heart."

But they haven't done the one thing that matters most: allow him to experience real, meaningful consequences to keeping his heart closed.

You don't hold a man accountable by staying with him so long as he's unwilling to open his heart, or even learn how.

So that's the vegetarian meat of it. I know this may open up more questions than it answers. In the end, these practices help you stay connected to your own heart, whether or not your man makes the difficult journey himself, from his head to his heart.

If he does find his way to meeting you there, all the delicious better for everyone. If he doesn't, or he remains closed to even learning how … well, just keep listening to your own precious heart.

Because your own heart will always show you the way.

 ## 52

THE SEXIEST 3 WORDS
A MAN CAN SAY TO A WOMAN

"I love you." (nope)
"You look beautiful." (nope)
"Let's go shopping!" (depends how you say it, but still, no)
"How's your mother?" (no, this will just make her suspicious)

Those are all nice to say, and many women will likely want at least occasionally to hear those things from their partner. But none of those by themselves will necessarily have her soften all warm-putty-like into your hairy masculine arms.

The three sexiest words I'm referring to speak to primal forces within both men and women. An archetypal trip wire, these eight letters strung together can trigger a man's spine to straighten and make a woman swoon.

I wish I could say I figured this one out by myself, but a lady friend had to point this out. Once she did, I looked back to my own intimate relationships and saw overwhelming evidence for her case everywhere.

We were having coffee when she started telling me about her new boyfriend. He was refined and kind, loving and intelligent. He was a creative artist, and an accomplished one at that. She felt him a good man and she was happy. Then she told me about the first morning they woke up together, and that's when she really lit up during our conversation.

She has a dog. Normally the dog gets her up early to go pee outside when she's still in comatose denial of an outside world. On this particular morning, when the dog woke her up as usual, her new beau opened his eyes, looked at her and with nary a hesitation, issued the most magical three-word spell she could recall ever hearing from a man. She said these words slid from his masculine mouth smooth as a river stone and strong as steel (that's my interpretation of what she said). She swooned. She relaxed. Under his sudden spell she felt herself completely protected and cherished by this man's love.

"I got this."

That's all he said.

"I'm going to take on this uncomfortable mission-oriented task because that's how I can best offer my masculine gift right now while honoring your delicious gift of feminine energy to my life. I will demonstrate my deep commitment to your care by ensuring you can stay warm under the covers and linger in this moment of blissful embodied reverie."

He actually only said the first three words. That whole second paragraph is my rough translation as I believe my friend heard it.

But first he said it. Then he actually did it. She was so impressed you'd think he bought her the Eiffel Tower. All he did was walk her dog.

We live in an age when women are empowered to care for themselves like never before. Which ain't a bad thing. An adult woman should be able to care for herself. I watched my two moms doing just that throughout my childhood, and so I grew up mostly thinking women were just supposed to endlessly "I got this" for themselves.

My two moms (married to my two fathers) held my two childhood worlds together. I watched my mom and step-mom, two brilliant, strong women, communicate "I got this" in countless ways to my dad, my step-father, and to me. Working women with big visions for life, they never seemed to "need" a man, which I took to mean no real woman needs a man.

I inevitably turned that model of woman into the model of my ideal mate: A woman who never needs me.

Growing up a "western man" in this modern world, I've received the message in countless ways that women are my equal in every way – and I say that's a good thing, from a certain perspective. Women *are* equal to men in terms of inherent human worth and value. They *should* have every legal right that any man has.

However, my understanding of sex equality completely overlooked certain ways my more feminine female partners and I were genuinely different. We yearned differently, meaning we experienced the world in rather different ways, even wanting different things from each other. For example, just holding a woman and making love with her is often a different experience for me than it is for my partners.

I don't embrace a woman to feel safe in her arms. When I embrace her I feel strong in my body, masterful even, as though I'm living my purpose by wrapping her up safe and protected within my steady arms. My female partners, in contrast, have often expressed that's what they love most about being in my embrace: the experience of feeling safe, physically and emotionally, that they can relax in knowing they're protected in that one moment from the tiresome chaos of the world. It's as if we both journeyed from very different worlds to secretly rendezvous in this one moment of exquisite embrace.

Failing too often to account for such differences, I have struggled in most of my intimate relationships with women. Clearly a contributing factor has been my inability to step up in all kinds of situations and say to my partners—often even to myself—*"I got this."*

Before I wade too deep into controversial waters, let me clarify that what I'm exploring is less about man-woman and more about masculine-feminine. Any foray into masculine-feminine dynamics risks offending those who hear those terms being used synonymously. I don't mean to do that. What I'm pointing at holds for all couples—hetero, gay, or otherwise—in which one partner carries more masculine energy and the other carries more feminine. Sometimes those energies can switch back and forth between partners. I invite you to see through to the deeper rhythms I'm exploring, beyond the details of who has what body parts.

I simply want to convey that when I look back through my life, I see far too often that I left my more core-feminine partners to fend for themselves in ways large and small. From making them decide where we should eat to running away when they were stressed emotionally and I hadn't the capacity to love them through it, I failed too often to step up and say, *"I got this."*

Which just means I consistently failed to convey, *"Baby, I invite you to relax and trust that all will be well because I have the strength, the discipline, the fortitude and the vision – and at the very least the unwavering perseverance – to hold us through this moment of discomfort and steward us safely to new ground where we will experience a brighter moment of ease together."*

Ok, so that's a bit poetic when we're talking about walking the dog or deciding where to eat. And sometimes our partners will genuinely want to bear their own burdens, or bear them equally alongside us, or even bear ours for us. I'm painting in broad strokes here.

Say to yourself a few times: *"I got this."*

How does that feel in your body?

Do you feel your chest rise a bit, your breathing deepen, your backbone straighten? Do you come alive and start looking around the room for some challenge to take on?

Or do you prefer imagining someone say it to you? Does the thought of your partner whispering it to you all sexy-like make your body soften and your heartbeat quicken? Does it set your yearning alight?

Truth is, I've always wanted a woman who can take care of herself. Which seems healthy to me. Any mature adult should be able to take care of themselves in the modern world. I don't want a partner who expects me to run around telling her *"I got this"* so she can stay in bed all day and eat spicy Cheetos (except maybe on her birthday, or Mother's Day). That would just be exhausting for me and eventually frustrating for her. I'm not Superman. She's not helpless.

Still, there's something deeply compelling about the idea of being with a woman who can fully take care of herself, and who enjoys allowing me to take care of her anyway.

"I got this."

 53

THE SEXIEST 3 WORDS
A WOMAN CAN SAY TO A MAN

I know what you're thinking. But no.

"Let's have sex" are actually NOT the three sexiest words a woman can say to a man.

They might be the most instantly sex-inducing words she can say, but they're not the sexiest. Sexy is about way more than sex.

If you've read my companion article, The Sexiest 3 Words a Man Can Say to a Woman, you might infer that the three sexiest words a woman can say to a man are: *"YOU get this."*

Again, no.

A man connected to his masculine essence won't generally find it sexy to be ordered around by an intimate partner. Most women don't find a man who will follow their orders very sexy, either.

There's nothing sexy about a doormat, or walking on one. (dominatrixing is outside the scope of this exploration)

The three words I'm talking about – whether she whispers them in his ear or writes them in sharpie on a pizza box top and subtly pushes them into his view – can quickly flood his spinal cord with backbone fluid, snap his shoulders square, and unfurl his superman cape.

They're so potent that a man freshly armed with these words may suddenly find himself inspired to leap tall buildings in a single bound and rescue kittens from trees. They definitely inspire him to show up for her, whatever that looks like in the moment.

These three words make him feel deeply sexy.

These three words *make everyone feel sexy.*

For when he truly receives them, they trigger his primal masculinity, strengthening him with resolve, deepening his commitment to purpose. For her to authentically offer them, she must allow herself to relax and surrender ambition to control how this moment flows, which is enlivening to her sensual feminine essence. With these three words, she is essentially saying, *"I know you've got this."*

The three sexiest words a woman can say to a man are: *"I trust you."*

I don't trust you: A long-term relationship I attempted to pull off in my 30s had ongoing core problems around trust.

For five years, I ached for her trust in me, but she would never fully offer it. She never admitted this, but she was still angry over her ex-husband's sexual betrayal, and I was paying the price. In fairness, though, I wasn't yet a man fully worthy of her trust. Early in our relationship, before we had even agreed on being monogamous, she caught me in a lie which antagonized her betrayal wound. My lie set fire to her toxic waste pond. Disregarding what would soon become a raging hellfire, we moved in together.

Since we're talking sexy here, I'll share that we had exquisite sex. Lots of it. Delicious physical pleasure. Truly. Lots. But without trust, neither one of us allowed ourselves to be truly vulnerable with each other. Neither of us felt safe to surrender to the blissful exchange of love energy that flows between two people in a healthy intimacy, which requires vulnerability.

She gave me her body during sex, but often withheld her true heart. She didn't feel emotionally safe with me, so she rarely offered the immense love inside her that ached for expression in our relationship.

We looked sexy together on the outside, and we had physical pleasure, but we felt awful in our depths.

"True sexy" arises from a person's depths. True sexy is about being deeply empowered in your entire being; it's about moving through the world connected and aligned to your deepest truth. Stepping fully into the brilliance of you who are, mind, body, heart, and soul, in this very moment. Author Janne Robinson said it best when she responded to my Facebook post on the subject of sexy with these words: *"I feel sexiest when I am living who I really am."*

In my relationship, we did not feel safe to give the gift of our true selves to each other. She was persistently afraid I would abandon her, so she held back the gift of her trust and her full love. I was persistently frustrated by her attempts to control me, so I resisted completely cherishing her and showing up for her in countless ways.

Resentment seethed during the 23 hours a day when we weren't having sex. We were often either dodging blame or flinging it at each other like monkey feces. It was not a sexy experience.

When a woman trusts a man, she's trusting in the gift of his masculinity to protect and provide strength and effective direction in this moment. She is letting go of worry, allowing herself to open and soften any walls around her sensual, feeling heart. She melts into vulnerability and offers the expression of her true self in this moment.

To be told, *"I trust you,"* by a woman is to be told:

"I trust that you will hold me and everything I care about as infinitely precious; that you will act to protect and cherish my life, my heart, as well as the lives and hearts of those I care about: my children, my mothers and my sisters, too, for our hearts are all one. I also trust that you will be a place of steadfast strength I can anchor to when I might otherwise be overcome by the turbulent winds of this ever-changing moment. I offer my real self to you, relaxed and vulnerable, confident that your best self will keep me safe as I do."

Or something like that.

A woman's willingness to be her true, unguarded self is an essential aspect of her feminine gift, for her femininity shines through when she relaxes into herself.

Whether the warm glow emanating from her lit-up eyes, the sensual swing in her confident step or the raw unbridled truth in her authentic sharing, her femininity is wildly attractive to many men. It even compels men to step deeper into their own innate masculinity.

In other words, these three words can inspire a man to claim his birthright as a responsible, loving, ethical being who champions all life and passionately serves the greater good. They routinely inspire him to not let her down. And every man wants to make his woman proud of him.

Imagine a world in which all men are genuinely worthy of any woman's trust. Also imagine also a world in which every woman is so deeply connected to the wondrous being she already is – whole enough, worthy enough, lovable enough – that her trust in herself allows her to relax and offer her authentic feminine gifts freely to her partner because she can now trust him to always be whomever he chooses to be.

Damn, that would be one sexy planet!

 54

3 STEPS TO A
LIFE-CHANGING APOLOGY

Apologies are easy.

It's swallowing that jagged little pill of pride that's hard.

A genuine apology (with no sneaky agenda) can transform the dynamic in any relationship from a charged adversarial stand-off into the elegant dance of partnership.

A wonderful karma-fixer, an apology can avert years of upset and disconnection.

Too often, though, excuses deny the cathartic power of apology. There's some reason why we did whatever we did that thing that upset another, and that reason stops us from taking responsibility: *"It's the reason's fault!"* we say, *"not mine."* On rare occasions, that reason might even be a good one. Maybe I really did drop my phone in the toilet and that's why I never called you back.

Whether your excuse is accurate or absurd, it doesn't matter. We all act unskillfully at times. Sometimes we simply react poorly to another's cringe-inducing behavior, which makes it doubly hard to apologize:

"Yes, I realize I got angry and dumped chocolate pudding all over her clean carpet, but she should apologize first for what she said that made me do it!"

It can feel like being the hockey player who winds up alone in the penalty box after throwing the second punch. The referee didn't see the first punch thrown by the other guy, so he skates free while I fume. I was in a relationship like that once. To my endless frustration, that girlfriend played both the blind referee and the sucker-puncher who skated free. So unfair, I thought at the time.

Here's the thing:

Whether your reason is awesome or absurd, it doesn't matter.

We all act unskillfully at times.

In the face of some circumstance or trigger, we do something. That something may be effective and inspiring, like Neo in The Matrix stopping bullets and helicopters! Sometimes, though, what we do is simply unhelpful and actually exacerbates situations despite our best intentions.

I believe we are all innocent in our ignorance. If we knew how to do relationships better, we would do them better. We only react poorly in any situation, or lash out and hurt people, when we are disoriented or hurting inside. You can't say with anger, "I hate you!" when you feel good.

If we knew how to move perfectly through every situation, we would do so.

But we don't.

Thus life giveth unto us … the apology.

Breakdowns are powerful gateways to breakthroughs. The bigger the breakdown, the bigger the potential breakthrough. Truly, it is our saving grace that big breakdowns can be powerful gateways to big breakthroughs.

I once worked with a relationship-coaching client whose relationship suddenly entered into a major breakdown in the middle of our work together. Disheartened and distraught, he called me from the hotel he'd retreated to the night before. The details of his situation aren't important; essentially he and his partner were triggered by actions from the other that quickly sent them running in opposite directions for cover as if war had just broken out.

As he sat in the quiet calm of his hotel room, we explored how he could navigate this breakdown in a way that might tease out a meaningful breakthrough. I knew this moment held massive potential for deeper understanding, kindness, connection and love between him and his wife. I also knew a real apology was the only way forward, but he couldn't yet see his way there.

So I shared these three steps to offering an apology that could quickly turn everything around:

Step 1 – "I see me"

I see what I did that was unskillful. I see how events overwhelmed my capacity to be good with you, and I reacted poorly as a result. I may have done the best I could at the time, or at least the only thing I knew how to do, and I'm sure I could have done it better. I'm sorry.

"I see me" is about taking ownership. Apologies crash when we embed them with this idea: *"I only did X because you did Y."* That's not an apology; it's a passive-aggressive excuse. It still blames my partner, which makes me a victim.

"I see me" means I see how I didn't keep my heart open to you; how I failed to respect, honor, cherish, appreciate or love you.

"I see me" means I see how I didn't keep my heart open to you; how I failed to respect, honor, cherish, appreciate or love you.

In Step 1, I take responsibility for my role in the breakdown. It may be hard to find my role, but no matter who did what, I can always find it if I look close enough. After all, I still threw the second punch.

Step 2 – "I see you"

I can finally see what you really wanted from me: safety, love, assurance, reliability, presence, participation, kindness, love. I see that I did not give to you. Regardless of my reasons, and regardless whether it's even my responsibility to give it to you, I didn't. I see the pain you felt as a result. Whatever you did to deal with that pain, I can see your innocence in that.

"I see you" is about compassion and empathy, which build a bridge right into your partner's heart.

By acknowledging my partner's experience, without making her wrong for it, I let her know she's safe with me. It's my way of saying, whatever you're going through, I can be with you through that. I know I failed when the breakdown happened, but I'm learning, too. I needed some space to really see myself, to really see you.

We're all learning how to be masterful in life. We won't quite nail it every time (or even most of the time).

When my awareness of self and other is limited, I react as if everything is happening TO me. I live in victimhood.

As I grow in awareness and learn to see more quickly what really happens in myself and others when a breakdown occurs, I can address the situation with a sincere apology that moves us more quickly towards healing.

It's been said we can either be right or we can be happy.

The breakdown is only there to show us what we couldn't see before. Eventually, with awareness, we can immediately give whatever love, attention, presence, kindness, clarity a situation needs. That's all that waits on the breakthrough side of a breakdown, anyway.

Which brings me to Step 3 …

Step 3 – "I love you"

I so absolutely love and adore you. I'm here, ready and willing to work through whatever comes our way. In fact, I love you so much that if your deepest truth is that you want to be alone now, I'll leave you alone. That's how much I love you.

"I love you" is the golden capstone on a gorgeous apology. It's the exhilarating ecstasy we melt into at the moment of breakthrough.

I affirm my commitment to loving and honoring my partner, assuring her that regardless where we go from here, I'm committed to love. It's not easy for one to keep a hard heart in the presence of such a commitment (though it's not impossible, if the wounds are deep enough).

Perhaps the most precious gift we can ever receive from another is to be fully seen and loved by them. If so, then the most precious gift we can give another is to fully see and love them, too.

During a breakdown, we fail to see the truth of each other, and of ourselves. Instead we only see our stories which are often just projections of our fears and wounds. We go blind and stop loving. War reigns.

A great apology can end that war, simple as 1-2-3.

 ## 55

STOP THIS TRAGIC CYCLE
IN YOUR RELATIONSHIP

(Note: this essay describes a phenomenon that happens in all relationships, straight or otherwise. It's a masculine-feminine dynamic, not a man-woman dynamic.)

I've discovered a tragic cycle in intimacy:

Woman routinely lets man know he's "not enough" (doesn't feel enough, not emotional enough, not expressive enough, often combined with he can't get it/do it right). Having no idea how to please her, he gives up, shrinks his hobbled feelings even more until he shuts down altogether.

Relationship over.

On the flip side:

Man often tells woman she's "too much" (too expressive, too emotional, too unpredictable, too whatever). So she learns to shrink herself hoping that will make him love her, until eventually, tragically, she then also becomes "not enough" (for him OR for herself).

Relationship over.

Here's an idea to end the insanity:

WOMAN, give the man space to feel however he feels (or doesn't feel).

Don't blame or leave him because you're frustrated he doesn't know how to touch his feelings. He's been taught since he was a boy not to touch those things, except with the little pole between his legs.

I know it's hard for you when he doesn't feel like you feel, but feeling is your feminine mastery, not his. Of course he's capable, it just ain't his primary nature and he's not as practiced as you.

But you can lead the way for him into discovery of his own feelings, NOT by admonishing him for not being as "good at feeling" as you are, but by honoring your own feelings fully, offering them to the relationship honestly while also reassuring him repeatedly that he's fully free to feel whatever he feels, too (or doesn't feel).

MAN, stop telling her she's too much for you (or the world).

Yes, I know she often is too much for your more still nature. She knows she often is, too. But do your damn best to love her as she colors your relationship with all the expressive flavors of her wild heart. That's what attracted you to her in the first place. Don't tell her to squash it now that she's in your presence all the time! Don't make her more masculine like you!! She's not your roommate or your buddy. She's your woman!!

Let her decorate your life with whatever sparkly, capricious, confounding ways delight her. Reassure her repeatedly that you love the unending mystery of her, even when her mystery frustrates the hell out of you. Because if you're loving her right, she will frustrate your mind, right into heaven!

In the end, I believe the best any of us can ever hope for is a partner who's simply willing to keep showing up, who's willing to learn how to do this wild dance of opposites with at least a little more grace and tenderness and flow and laughter and love than we experienced yesterday.

Doesn't that sound amazing?

 56

THE ONE MISUNDERSTANDING THAT ROUTINELY RUINS RELATIONSHIPS

There's a terrible phenomenon that destroys otherwise good relationships. I call it the *"Relationship Death Gap."*

This is what happens:

The more masculine partner in the relationship – the one who prioritizes rational thinking over emotional expression – is ok with something, could be anything. Maybe he (or she) wants to go out with friends even though his partner is sick in bed with the flu. Or maybe he wants to invite his ex-girlfriend to his birthday party. Or maybe a million other scenarios.

Whatever it is, his more feminine partner – who's more feeling-oriented and emotionally connected than he is – feels upset about it. If her upset isn't immediately understood and validated, she gets even more upset!

He may not have actually done anything yet, but just the fact that he doesn't validate her upset and instead defends his logic as justification for being ok with whatever the thing, well … that's even more upsetting to her.

Even if he finally agrees to stay home or not invite his ex-girlfriend hardly matters, particularly if he does so just to get his partner off his back and not because he actually understands her feelings about it. She remains upset, anyway.

Now he's pissed, too. Doubly so. Because not only is he angry at himself for giving in to something that doesn't make sense to him, he's extra frustrated that she's still not happy after she got what she said she wanted.

Sound familiar?

This is the Relationship Death Gap, and it kills relationships slowly.

Here's what's actually going on, and what to do about it:

Naturally, his logic works for him. His reasons make perfect sense to him. He knows his ex-girlfriend is no threat. He knows he loves and is committed to his partner. He even believes a man who can stay friends with an ex is the mark of a generous, loving man. He thinks his woman should be proud to be with such a man! And, he sees the countless things he does that prove his love for her! He sees no reason for her to worry or object!

Yet none of his matters to her. Her past experiences – and biology – may cause her to feel insecure about an ex. She may not feel genuinely, fully considered in his logic.

What's worse, if he can't validate her feelings because his reasons make more sense to him than her reasons for being upset, now she feels unsafe with him because she can't trust that he truly cares about her feelings, which she experiences as not caring about her!

He sees what he sees. She feels what she feels. She can't convince him to change his thinking. He can't calm her emotions with his logic. The more they both try, the more defiant they both get.

This is how the same argument plays itself out for months, even years, as the Relationship Death Gap grows.

It's maddening to the more masculine partner who thinks what happened is long over. He might still think the offense was only imagined, anyway, yet as long as his more feminine partner continues to feel that her emotional experience has never been fully embraced by him, the disconnect grows … until no connection remains at all.

Two good people swallowed into the Relationship Death Gap.

So, how do you close the gap? It's simple. Just not easy, because you gotta suspend your viewpoint for a moment and dive into your partner's experience.

1. The more masculine partner needs to embrace her feelings, even if they don't make logical sense to him.

In fact, if you can give up needing her feelings to make sense to you – and I mean *ever* – just learn to accept that her feelings are real for her, and communicate that you support her feeling whatever she feels, most things will go much better for both of you.

All she wants is to be validated in what she feels, to know you don't think she's crazy. And I know her reasons for being upset might make her seem crazy to you, but so long as you orient towards her as though she's crazy and you fail to embrace her feelings, she'll feel that too, and she's gonna be hell for you. She'll either get louder or shut down altogether, and you don't want either of those outcomes.

2. The more feminine partner needs to try to understand his logic, even though it may hurt.

Accept that he's sharing his reality, and in his reality he has good intentions and never wants for you to hurt. If you think he's lying or that he does want to hurt you, or he just won't ever take responsibility for how he affects you, you probably shouldn't be with him. But if you do trust he genuinely wants to be a good man for you, then assure him you really understand that; that you know he never means to harm you. Because that's almost certainly what he's aching for you to understand. Tell him you can see his good, or at least innocent, intentions, and he'll feel seen and understood. His resistance will relax because he no longer feels the need to keep proving himself to you.

I know both of you are worried you're going to lose something: Your freedom. Validation. Connection. Your identity. Your sanity. But notice how your resistance to embracing each other's reality is already causing you to lose all that.

You've got to understand you two are never going to experience life the same way all the time. Tiny gaps of misunderstanding will continue opening up between you for the rest of your lives together, at least if you're committed to being real with each other.

The trick is not to get rid of gaps forever, but to learn how to close them quickly before they drain your intimacy of all affection, care and even respect for each other.

What's surprising is that as you learn to embrace each other's reality without denying your own, often whatever you were fighting about just stops being a thing because you stop being enemies. Your partner trusts you to have their back.

Which doesn't necessarily make the ex-girlfriend at the party decision obvious, but if you're the more feminine partner, you just might be surprised how inspired he is to really take care of you once he gets that you genuinely appreciate his point of view.

If you're the more masculine partner, you'll be surprised how much she lets go and trusts you, even follows your lead because she feels that you're going to really care about her feelings whatever may come.

 57

WHY CHALLENGING YOUR WOMAN NEVER WORKS (WHAT TO DO INSTEAD)

One recent Saturday my lady and her mom spent the morning baking chocolate banana bread in our kitchen.

They went to the store together, bought all the ingredients together, came home and made that scrumptious bread alongside a delightful breakfast feast of which I was the sole non-contributing beneficiary. I didn't even have to grab a napkin or pull a fork from a drawer.

Shortly after pulling the bread from the oven, lovely Silvy brought some to me in my office (I was working that morning). Smelling all sweet and lit up in the joy of cooking with her mom, Silvy smiled as she cupped the bread with one hand to ensure no crumbs would spill on my keyboard and with her other hand delicately placed a warm slice of chocolate heaven into my mouth.

My first thought was, *"Yummy, chocolate!"*

My second thought was, *"It's a bit dry."*

For so long, I've been so intimately identified with working to triumph over life's challenges, fix life's (unending) sea of problems, and address any little thing that's *juuuuust* a bit off so I and the people I love can …. well, I suppose so we can experience an absolutely perfect and problem-free life. Although I've never figured out what such a life would actually offer.

Curiously, the actual problem I notice is that by constantly focusing on fixing life's apparent problems, I just end up living in a world of unending problems. Thus I daily overlook all that's already working wonderfully around me. It's as if my comfort zone requires problems. So even where they don't exist, I create them. Even in my writing – including this piece – it seems I (mostly) only know how to frame life as a challenge to overcome.

After working with thousands of men, women, and couples in my coaching practice, I believe this is the single biggest problem facing most men (and many women):

We overlook (ignore) all that's working and favorable in our lives, and instead focus on anything (everything) that seems (to our minds) not to be. Which has devastating consequences, particularly in intimate relationships.

THE MAGIC 5:1 RATIO

After decades studying couples in an actual laboratory environment, The Gottman Institute discovered an essential 5 to 1 ratio: Five positive interactions between you and your partner are necessary for every one negative or neutral interaction if you want your relationship to genuinely succeed.

How many couples have you seen consistently interact so positively with each other in front of you (when they're likely on their best behavior; never-mind behind closed doors!)?

How often have you hit that positive ratio?

Consider: masculine energy rises in the face of challenge while feminine energy rises in response to praise. (Reminder: masculine does not mean man, and feminine does not mean woman; by masculine I essentially mean "fix-it mode" and by feminine I essentially mean "the flow of love between two people.")

Author David Deida first enlightened me about the dance of complementary masculine and feminine energies many years ago. Not only do his descriptions fit perfectly with Gottman's golden love ratio, I see the direct evidence of this in the couples I coach and in my own relationship experiences, too.

I've always required challenge to feel inspired and excited by whatever I'm doing. I've always needed my work, my opponent on the sports field, even the woman I'm with to be sufficiently (though not overwhelmingly) challenging as to offer my masculine-oriented fix-it mind compelling puzzles to solve. Otherwise, I grow bored and disconnected from the work, the game, the woman, and seek out new challenges elsewhere.

Which means I want to be challenged by those around me, particularly when they see I'm not living up to my full potential in some way – even if I merely failed to nail that banana bread recipe. Of course I want to be challenged respectfully; no man enjoys being criticized any more than any woman does.

However, challenge isn't what inspires feminine "love flow" between two people. Only praise does that.

Most of us aren't overtly taught praise, and we rarely see it modeled by our parents towards each other (or politicians, business leaders, or most anyone else in our problem-focused society).

We more likely learn to focus on what isn't working, even if for the well-intentioned purpose of trying to fix it. Which might work in a factory of machines, but it's only always a hurtful (and completely futile) approach to intimacy.

I know I don't praise my woman nearly enough. I'm so identified with overcoming challenge – *"we need more money"*; *"the dog requires too much attention"*; *"the bread isn't moist enough"* – that I don't tell her nearly enough how extraordinary she is, how kind and generous and brilliant and talented and exquisite and gorgeous she is, and how profoundly lucky I am to wake up next to her every day.

Like many men, I too often overlook what an absolute privilege it is to love my woman. A privilege that one day, even if by death, I will not have anymore *for all eternity.*

Until that day, I get to wake up next to an exquisite creature, the sweet-scented woman I've been waiting for who challenges me in all the right ways, who intrigues and excites me, frustrates, inspires, confuses, and in the end always utterly delights me. Each day is another day I get to deep dive into the blissful infinity of her dark eyes which consistently gaze back at me with an adoration that easily obliterates any (imagined) problem I might be believing in that day.

Reality check: "real problems" are mostly imagined. I certainly have challenges. And I regularly experience situations that occur as difficult. For example, just a week ago, I had foot surgery. A secondary infection has infiltrated the wound, further delaying my healing and ability to walk normally. I could focus on what's gone "wrong" with my healing, or I could focus on the more empowering, more praise-worthy reality that I live in a time where medicines and doctors can help me not lose my foot – or my life – due to a simple infection. I could focus on the fact that I live with an exquisite companion who will do most anything to ensure I get the proper health care I need to heal well.

In fact, no matter what (awful) experiences may ever be happening around me, I can always bring my focus to the simplest things that are working beautifully in this moment to support me being alive:

I am breathing air that doesn't care whether I've brushed my teeth, and I can rest my tired butt on a chair, sofa, bed, or just earthy ground that doesn't care if I washed my shorts and never asks anything in return. (Thanks to my old friend, singer Ash Ruiz, for these simple yet extraordinary gratitudes)

Even in the midst of my biggest breakdowns – which usually just means I've suddenly conjured up some massive imaginary problem my mind has no answer for – when I turn my focus to even the smallest working aspects of my life, praise becomes near effortless.

Because everything suddenly turns into a gift.

Even arguing with my partner or having an infected foot becomes a kind of bonus-experience that lives on top of everything else working so perfectly in my life to even allow me such experiences in the first place. I still take the actions necessary to heal my foot, but now I do so in a mindset of gratitude for having a foot at all.

Now all the love and sweetness my woman and her mom baked into every browned fiber of that chocolate banana bread can just ooze deliciousness all over my fix-it-focus moment of concern about its moisture content. Because you should know: I devoured her delicious bread with gusto.

I'm profoundly grateful this extraordinary woman delights in feeding me. I'm grateful for her in my life, and for all our wild adventures both passed and yet to come.

When I focus on what's working, like a simple warm, chocolatey surprise on my tongue, praise becomes effortless … to my woman's utter delight. And thus to mine.

 58

YOUR GOOD INTENTIONS ARE (MOSTLY) IRRELEVANT WHEN YOUR PARTNER IS HURTING

I never understood why the women I loved were so often angry at me.

My intentions were always good, and my heart always in the right place. I certainly never *wanted* to hurt anyone, least of all the woman I was trying my damndest to love.

Then one day, in the painful midst of yet another lover-spat going nowhere fast, I finally got it: I am wickedly skilled at dismissing a woman's hurt feelings as invalid on the grounds of my good intentions. In my certainty that she's simply misread the situation, I dismiss her reality as invalid, and that would infuriate most anyone … including me!

Here are things I'd typically say when stubbornly refusing to take responsibility for how my actions (or words) negatively impacted my partner:

"Stop focusing on the negative; see the bigger picture (silver lining) instead."

"You're a grownup, responsible for your own feelings. Don't blame your choice (to suffer) on me!"

"If you really understood my (good) intentions you wouldn't be so upset."

Yikes. While those words are well-intentioned, possibly even speak truth, they're not helpful. They're verbal uppercuts thrust towards her when her upset threatens the shame, or the arrogance, lurking within me.

What I later understood a woman was often wanting from me when she feels hurt by something I've done or said is simply comfort and reassurance. She doesn't want to be shown the "errors" in her thinking. She wants to feel emotionally connected and safe with me again.

Yet my responses never created connection or safety. What they did instead is merely confirm for her that I don't understand her world at all. I always thought I was doing my partner a great service by helping to rid her of "negative" feelings or thoughts using perspective and logic (my own, to be sure). I didn't understand that perspective and logic were only helpful *after* she felt fully seen and acknowledged by me.

Today, after many years coaching couples (and 30 years personal experience) I've found that perhaps the biggest obstacle to conflict resolution in intimacy is learning to understand that:

1. My desire (intention) to not hurt my partner is never the determining factor as to whether they're actually hurt, and

2. Acknowledging and validating their experience, feelings, hurt does not necessarily mean I must also see things the same way or agree on the root cause (e.g. who/what is at fault).

As we get better at responding to a partner's upsets with curiosity and deep listening – and stop fighting on the hill of well-intentioned righteousness – relationship gets better.

Disagreements don't spiral into verbal-emotional combat. Misunderstandings and miscommunications don't morph into all-night cage matches. Instead, moments of disconnect actually get repaired, damn near immediately.

A PRACTICE

Next time your partner (or close friend, family member) communicates an upset towards you, before you respond, take a deep breath.

Then take 10 more deep breaths.

I know, chances are, they're not communicating *skillfully*. They may be blaming or accusing you of something you don't believe yourself guilty of. They may even be attempting to shame you, which is neither kind nor helpful. Harshness never serves love.

Nonetheless, consider that it's likely they have rarely, if ever, felt deeply seen, heard, or validated by the world around them, or even by the ones they love most. For even just a moment can you acknowledge their hurt, their upset, their pain?

Even if you don't agree with their conclusions or reasons for their upset, can you simply acknowledge this is real for them?

"I really get that this is upsetting for you. I can clearly see you're hurting and want you to know I accept this is real for you."

Tempting as I know it is, for now, leave out the part about disagreeing with them. That only serves to reinforce their sense of disconnect from you.

Stay with them in their pain, even just a few minutes. If they persist with harshness – blame or shame – or you just find that you just don't have the patience or capacity to sit with them through this, then consider getting professional support. You're not supposed to figure this out alone.

When my partner and I run into the walls that protect our own deep wounds and we cannot hear or see each other, we get professional help – and she's a marriage and family therapist and I'm a relationship coach!

If you want a thriving relationship, however, you must figure out that your words and actions can still hurt your partner, despite your best intentions, and that validating their experience is not the same as agreeing with it. Learn this, and intimate relationship will change forever for you, for the *massive* better.

 59

THE MOST ESSENTIAL (AND OVERLOOKED) BOUNDARY FOR HEALTHY RELATIONSHIPS

A few years ago, I was shocked to discover I'd spent a lifetime (unknowingly) allowing one especially critical boundary to be violated by the women I loved, over and over.

Naturally, I routinely violated this same boundary for them, too.

Had I been aware (and able to stand for this boundary) I'm convinced! I would have been able to actually enjoy relationships, rather than fear them as the nightmares they inevitably became.

Sadly, it didn't occur to me that I – a man – should even have boundaries, except the "obvious" ones of course. For the shallow-masculine world around me insisted there were basically only 3 ways a woman could violate me:

1. She cheats on (lies to) me
2. She disrespects (rejects) me
3. She takes tangible resources (money, things, time) from me without my permission.

That's it. Otherwise, I was completely sold into the (absurd) idea that a man is supposed to be tough, invulnerable, invincible, able to "handle" (whatever that means) anything difficult that comes his way …. least of all a woman!

Boundaries? Women need boundaries. Not me! (so I thought)

Thus I swam for decades in the deep, mysterious oceans of intimate relationship, blinded and unprotected from all kinds of painful boundary violating behavior, from the subtly upsetting (testy mermaids nipping at my toes) to the excruciatingly painful (great white sharks roaring up from the depths to swallow me whole as I thrashed about desperate for survival!).

But there was one specific boundary violation that kept happening over and over, and I've seen it since, countless times working with couples as a Relationship Coach since 2013. This unassuming little sea creature has a thousand microscopic spiny needles that quietly inject poison into intimacy, rotting out from the inside all feelings of trust and safety.

This is that one boundary violation:

When one partner assumes, with near or complete certainty, that they know what the other is thinking or feeling, or what they should be thinking or feeling.

Today, a significant part of my couples coaching work is teaching people how to create and maintain healthy boundaries in ways that leave both partners feeling heard, honored, and respected. Whether I'm working with individuals or couples, we'll work through all variety of boundary issues, from porn to infidelity, from work-life imbalances and co-dependency, to commitment confusions and all the ways one might give their power away to the world around them.

But this one boundary violation shows up in every relationship dynamic.

Here are ways in which it emerged from the mouths of my past loved ones, and from my mouth, too:

> *"You don't really care about me."*
> *"You obviously don't want to spend time with me."*
> *"You clearly want to be with someone else."*
> *"You should never have done X because I sure wouldn't have done X!"*
> *"You obviously don't know what's best for you."*
> *"You are clearly not as spiritual/conscious/wise/mature as I thought you were."*
> *"You shouldn't feel X; it doesn't make any sense."*
> *"You only did X to satisfy your ego."*
> *"You don't care about X as much as I do."*

… and on and on.

Notice these all start with "You," though they can be cleverly disguised by the conniving ego as "I" statements, too: *"I don't feel like you care about me."* Regardless, they're all conclusive declarations that *"I know what you're thinking or feeling (or what you should be)."*

Here's a more revealing way of saying the same thing: *"I can't see, hear, or feel the real you right now because the conclusions I'm creating in my mind about you are in the way."*

How's that going to inspire connection? It can't, and never does.

What it more commonly does is incite defensiveness, confusion, anger, resentment, shut down, withdrawal, disconnection.

Today, I understand my partner (or I) would only ever say such things out of pain and fear, when she, herself, feels deeply unseen or heard; when she's desperate for loving reassurance that I will hold her experience/feelings/perspective as valid and won't leave her alone in the pain.

I never knew that before. It still sometimes crushes me to look into my past, to see with more mature eyes the anguished faces of women I was trying to love. I can see now both the anger and the sadness in their eyes, betraying a profound ache to feel seen and heard by me.

Yet in the face of desperate attempts to have certainty, by insisting they knew my agenda – my thoughts and feelings, my why's, my inner world – all I could ever do was react poorly, defensively arguing for the right to exist. As if my entire being would be swallowed up by their conclusions that I knew missed the mark.

Here is what I should have done, instead – an effective 2-step response that would have saved us both:

1. Respectfully, lovingly, stand up for this boundary:

"Please stop saying you know what is true for me (what I'm thinking, or what I'm feeling). I'm not going to continue this conversation until you stop, and allow me the space to have my own experience."

2. Offer the reassurance she's really seeking.

"I really get that you're hurt (upset, mad, scared, confused, etc.). I'm here with you, and we'll figure this out together."

Because I've been practicing this for years now, and teaching this to my clients, I know what can happen next: Genuine curiosity and moments of real connection.

A PRACTICE

Notice the next time someone – whether intimate partner, friend, colleague, or family member – makes an assertion that they know what you're thinking or feeling (or what you should be). This could reveal itself in a thousand ways:

"You should want to go to X with me."
"You clearly did X because you're inconsiderate/ignorant/
  ashamed/confused/insensitive …"
"You should feel ashamed/embarrassed/disgusted/happy/relieved.…"
"You should see this from X perspective."
"Why are you single?" (no one ever asks: *"Why are you in a relationship?"*)

To be sure, sometimes people can actually be helpful when offering different perspectives. Often, though, it's not string-free assistance they're offering; rather, they're attempting to enroll you in their own worldview so they don't feel so alone in it, themselves.

Regardless, if it doesn't feel helpful, don't attempt to defend yourself by trying to convince them of what you're thinking or feeling. Instead, simply ask them in this very moment not to assume they know what is (or should be) happening for you.

If you're not too emotionally charged, you might thank them for trying to offer insight (or whatever they're trying to offer), even as you stand up for this boundary.

I find acknowledging people for their good intentions, even if their execution be poor, goes a long way towards maintaining respect and partnership even through the most difficult of disagreements.

If you're the one being asked to stop, you could simply say, *"My apologies. I didn't mean to assume I know your inner world."*

Then get curious. Invite them to share what actually is going on for them, and trust they're speaking truth to the best of their capacity in that moment. If you can't trust that, it ain't likely to be a meaningful conversation, anyway! Ultimately, whichever end of this you're on, the point is to open up space for curiosity, for curiosity draws people together.

Curiosity creates connection. Drawing conclusions about each other tends to destroy it. Learning to honor this one boundary can profoundly improve the quality of your relationships. It sure has mine.

 **60**

STOP FIXING, START CONNECTING (AND SAVE YOUR RELATIONSHIP)

In a recent coaching session with a couple, I told a confused man whose wife was on the brink of leaving:

"She will follow you anywhere if you just stop trying to solve the 'problems of her' and instead practice connecting with her, acknowledging her experiences (curious to learn more), reassuring her you're with her through whatever difficulties."

When I said this, a wide, relaxed smile broke through like bright dawn on his wife's previously tense face.

"Yes! That's really all I want!" (her exact words)

Tragically, this runs counter to everything we men are taught. We're taught to solve problems, meet at the level of mind, fix things there. We know nothing of the body, emotions, feelings, being in heart. Yet a man's willingness to practice simply being with his partner's emotions – without judging, condemning, dismissing or *doing* anything to make them go away – dramatically increases his capacity to love immediately. Which increases the connection (flow of love) with his partner (which changes everything).

Ironically, most of those impossibly unsolvable "problems" he so desperately wants gone – which he doesn't think exist anyway and are just made up shit – magically disappear.

But we're never taught this. We're never taught that learning how to just *be with her* through whatever challenges, even when they seem to be caused by our actions and words, actually pulls us through faster.

Learning how to *be* with emotions and feelings – our partners and our own – without trying to make them go away can improve a relationship profoundly.

A PRACTICE

For the next 7 days, try just being with your partner's emotions, fully present, allowing, even embracing her (or his) experience.

No partner? Try being with your own.

Tip 1: Don't take their emotions personally. They aren't (really) about you, no matter how hard she tries to convince you they are.

Tip 2: Being with your partner's emotions will test your capacity to be with your own. Pay attention to (and practice being with) your own discomforts, too.

 # 61

THE INSPIRING STORY OF HOW I MET SILVY ... BY NOT TRUSTING FEAR

This is the inspiring true story of how I finally met the woman I waited a lifetime for – and how I met her in the middle of nowhere – because I trusted my heart over my fear.

It was magic. For when we met, I was all alone in a remote mountain valley cabin in the middle of Idaho. While I was there, I intentionally called her in. And she came quickly, within days. I later learned she had been calling me in, too.

It was in summer 2015, and I was feeling deeply called to leave Los Angeles where I had been living for a few years. I felt the deep yearning for a personal retreat, alone, to simply reconnect with myself, and to also finish writing my second book, <u>Tell The Truth,Let The Peace Fall Where It May.</u>

I was *aching* to leave Los Angeles. I felt it simmering in my bones. Life was calling me out of hectic city and into quiet nature to both finish my book and clear my city-frazzled head.

When two angels in Idaho offered me a cabin (complete with jacuzzi) nestled among the roots of a forest on the edge of a remote mountain valley, my heart knew it was time. I was giddy to go.

About 4 days before I planned to leave LA, I got a phone call from a casting agent. I'm not an actor, but living in LA and knowing folks can yield all kinds of curious opportunities, and this one leapt into my lap. American Express was doing a commercial and wanted to film an actual man (not a fictional character) who was going on an "eat-pray-love" kinda journey. The casting agent knew about my trip and wanted to submit me to the director. I was quickly chosen as one of 2 finalists for the commercial, which would pay $2,500 and expose me (and my work as a coach/author) to possibly millions of people.

There was one catch: I had to stay in LA at least another 2 weeks.

My worried, strategizing brain said:

"You can't miss this opportunity! You spend everything you make on rent, your business and working with your coach; you could really use $2500! Not only would it pay for this trip, but you would get exposure to countless potential clients! You can totally stay in LA a few more weeks, no problem!"

My wise, mysterious heart said:

"It's time to leave LA. Now. You feel it deeply. And although I can't yet show you how, I promise you will make more money if you go to Idaho now. Trust. Let go. Go."

When I thought of leaving immediately for Idaho, I noticed I felt light and excited all over my body. I also noticed I felt only heaviness when considering staying in LA for the commercial. *(Note: paying attention to how your body feels when faced with a decision is an essential power practice!)*

So I let go of the commercial and drove off into the unknown.

About 10 days later, after journeying through Nevada, Utah and Idaho visiting old friends and making new ones, I settled into that mountain cabin with plump black raspberries bursting off the bush outside my kitchen window, which overlooked a glorious green meadow where the sun would set late each night. I quickly settled in, and started writing the 10th – and final! – draft of my book. The road trip had been clearing my frazzled city-brain with each passing mile. Now, here I was with weeks of nothing stretching out before me, relaxed and ready to finish writing.

I had been there a week when, with a relaxed mind and a trickle of internet service, I decided to check for the first time in many months how many people were reading my blogs. I hadn't been checking those stats because, well, I was just so damn over worrying about the numbers. I just couldn't any longer care about such things back in LA. Not that I cared in this cabin, either.

But when I awoke that first quiet Sunday morning, my mind more rested and calm than it had been in a long time, I noticed a subtle whisper drifting through the cabin stillness like a butterfly.

"Just look and see," it spoke to me.

As I rose out of bed, I looked at my blog stats and saw that 1,000 people had already read "Choose Her Every Day (Or Leave Her)" that morning, a blog I had written months earlier. I also saw that only 500-1,000 people had been visiting my website on an average day, so I casually decided to just repost that blog again on my new Facebook author page thinking it might touch a few more people that day. Then I forgot about it, had breakfast and went for a mountain bike ride.

By the end of the day, I was shocked to see 40,000 people had read it. Thinking that was the height of it and by morning it'd be over, I was even more dumbstruck the next morning to see that over 120,000 people had read that blog before I'd even opened my eyes.

In the next 3 days, over 3 million people would read that blog. I didn't know it, but my life was about to change in the ways I had only so far dreamed of.

One night during that explosive week, I celebrated with a nighttime soak in the hot tub under a black sky sprinkled with stars like glitter. I drank a glass of celebratory champagne as candles lit a flickering ring around the patio deck, and I reflected:

"I have lived a blessed, magical life. I've adventured all over the world, trekked across deserts and oceans. I've lived in strange, foreign lands and slept in palaces and mansions and trailers and barns and everything in between. I've encountered myriad wondrous human characters and loved most of 'em. I've made money and lost it. I've loved many women and left or lost every one. Here I am once again, enjoying another magical moment ... but all alone."

I decided in that moment I was done journeying in this life alone.

I spoke aloud an intentional prayer, *"I am ready to start building a world with an extraordinary woman."* I watched these words float out through the steamy hot-tub haze towards an infinite black dome sky.

Over the next few days, my blog continued to explode and thousands of messages poured in. My courageous assistant, Gina, handled most of it (I had hired Gina on faith a year before by giving her $500 for a month's work when I only had $1500 to my name – another act of intuitive knowing despite my worried brain telling me I'm crazy).

Facebook friend-requests and new fans poured in by the thousands, too. One stood out. The day after my hot-tub revelation, I received a friend request from a dark-haired, dark-eyed woman named Silvy. She lived in LA, and we shared special friends, so I started a chat with her.

Expecting nothing, simply connecting, we chatted for a few minutes. Feeling inspired, my heart-ripped open by this magical moment, I vulnerably confessed my deep clarity that I was ready to share this wondrous life I'm so grateful for. I had absolutely zero idea I was actually typing this to my incoming life partner.

She would tell me months later my vulnerability was endearing. She was more accustomed to men who tried to impress her with money and success, who weren't willing to offer the simple truths of their hearts.

The chat lasted a few minutes, then it was over.

Over the next few months, I traveled to the Australian Outback and was consumed by all that viral-blog energy coming at me from everywhere. Silvy and I had a few missed encounters and didn't really connect again.

Then, two months after our first chat, stars again aligned and we were finally able to meet at a cafe near her sister's home. In the very moment we locked eyes across that cafe, I felt as though I was about to dive into the deepest ocean I'd ever known.

When we hugged hello seconds later, I dove in. Perhaps I fell in. I haven't stopped exploring her delicious depths since. This woman contains the whole universe inside her. There is no end to the mysteries that animate her and fascinate me. What most delights me about being with her is that – though I began loving her soon after we met – I find that I like her more and more, the more I discover of her.

As Silvy continues to sweep like springtime across the land of my deepest heart's dreams, I'm profoundly aware that I had to trust my heart's inner knowing and journey alone to the middle of nowhere to find the quiet place (within me) where I could finally discover her.

I told you it was pure magic.

Oh, and during the month this all happened, I made over $20,000. It was the most money I had ever made in one month. A few months later, I would make over $25,000 in one month.

Can you imagine? To think I almost traded a massive breakthrough in my writing career, more money than I've ever made and meeting the woman

I've waited a lifetime for … all for a $2500 credit card commercial and prolonged discontent.

Next time you're faced with choosing between trusting in fear or trusting in what would delight your authentic heart, remember my story. Fear might get you $2500, but it could cost you your biggest dream.

 62

ONE ESSENTIAL KEY TO RELATIONSHIP SUCCESS (DON'T TRUST YOUR CONCLUSIONS)

Not long ago, I just knew my relationship with my fiancé was over.

I saw it so clearly driving home one cloudy morning after having my Kia hybrid serviced. The night before, we'd descended into a painfully familiar argument we'd already had too many times before, though the specific details were often different.

Indeed, coaching couples these last many years has taught me that while the details of disagreements and arguments will often change, the fears at their core rarely do.

As I drove home to where she awaited, crystalline meditation music gently whispered through my car's new speakers, wrapping tightly around my heavy heart as my mind laid out its case:

"Bryan, the gap between her sensitivities and yours is too great to bridge. This keeps coming up. It's not going away. You'll only keep tormenting each other, even if innocently so, for as long as you stay. The kindest, most loving choice is to end things. Now."

Fragile tears began to pool in my eyes, blurring the road before me.

The conclusion was clear: We can't stay together.

The beautiful futures we had both envisioned flashed and crashed before me: our upcoming trip home to my family; our big, spacious someday-fantasy house with a big, stupid-friendly dog and a couple mini-me rugrats; our inspired visions to create relationship coaching programs, workshops and retreats to serve humanity's awakening to love …. hell, how can I even be a relationship coach anymore!?

How can I possibly help others create thriving relationships when I can't even keep alive my most important relationship with the extraordinary woman I've waited a lifetime for!?

The highway between me and the home we shared grew mercilessly shorter as everything I had built and dreamed of building imploded in my mind's eye.

Then this thought floated into my consciousness: *"Don't believe your conclusions."*

I recalled <u>A Course in Miracles</u>, a mystical book I tried reading 10 years ago with a previous girlfriend. That relationship was so persistently chaotic that we started fighting exactly halfway through the first sentence we read together, and so I quickly gave up reading it. That relationship was lost, too, though I did save the book.

"You are not afraid or worried for the reasons you think."

That's the fifth daily lesson in A Course in Miracles, which has 365 daily lessons.

On this fateful day, those enigmatic words would save my relationship from death by logical conclusion. For I saw that our relationship would indeed be over if I kept choosing to believe in my brain's logic – but that our relationship did not have to be over if I could simply stop believing in the imagined future my brain had me fearing.

One of the most common (and agonizing) dilemmas I see in my relationship coaching clients' lives is this: *"I'm damned if I do, damned if I don't."*

In other words, no matter what I do I'm screwed (and not in the ways I want to be)! If I choose to accept and live with what I think is happening, life will suck because I don't like it, yet if I choose NOT to accept and live with what is happening, life will also suck because it means I'll lose something important (love, companionship, validation, joy, etc.) …. Damned if I do, damned if I don't!

Here I was now facing that devil's choice: two impossible paths before me, each promising to devastate our lives.

"Don't believe your conclusions. Instead, feel what you're feeling."

We men don't feel our feelings nearly enough. We surely don't embrace them. Instead we usually act out our mental logic with little consideration for how anyone feels about our actions, thus damaging the emotional connection with our partners (and ourselves) over and over.

After all, if we can't connect to our own feelings, how can we possibly connect to anyone else's feelings? Thus we destroy love in the name of logic (our own) and outcome (the one we want).

Essentially, we destroy love to avoid feeling discomfort.

As I watched my windshield wipers rapidly whisking away the outdoor mist obscuring my drive, I resolved in that moment not to destroy our beautiful relationship, and our dreams, merely to avoid feeling the discomforting sadness and anger then arising in me. I refused to accept that *"damned if I do, damned if I don't"* was the best life could offer me.

After 20 minutes of eternity, I arrived home, sat her on the couch and said, *"I'm going to let myself be sad, even angry for now. Not with you, but with life. Because if I believe my conclusions, our relationship is over. I really don't want that. I love you, and I'm going to trust there must be bigger possibilities than what I can see. So for now, I'm just going to feel what I feel."*

She agreed and mostly understood, though her own fear tried for a few minutes to pry my thoughts from my mouth. I knew that wouldn't be fruitful, so I demurred, knowing we had a session with a brilliant therapist later that evening.

My fiancé and I are BOTH relationship coaches (she's also an Associate Therapist), and we regularly get support with other therapists and coaches. We know it's damn difficult even for the most aware and well-intentioned to create truly thriving, sustainable relationships when left to our own devices. We humans all have unhealed wounds, well-guarded blind spots, and clever egos all too eager to judge, conclude, and insist they know how things should be. When unchecked, all that can cause humans to make a damn fine mess out of love.

The road to hell is indeed paved with the best of intentions, and working with well-meaning couples who've made awful messes out of love has proved that to be true countless times over.

That evening, as our therapist helped guide us through that same argument, I held Silvy's hands, looked into her eyes, and reassured her we're in this together.

He then quietly whispered to us both:

"Always remember: You are never upset for the reasons you think are."

What?! Silvy's face lit up in surprise and my eyes bulged in disbelief.

He pointed out, almost as an aside, that we were both arguing about two very different things, that we weren't even having the same argument the other was having! (i.e. we were not angry for the reasons we thought we were.)

After our session, Silvy and I felt deeply reconnected. Though our "sensitivity gap" remained, our hope for the future was restored because we now had new tools to restore connection between us whenever this frightening gap reasserted itself.

This gap does still reassert itself from time to time.

Every relationship is the merging of two very different universes. Two people who have lived often vastly different lives, both fueled by ancient, primal masculine and feminine energies that can appear to completely oppose each other at times. We each bring an array of old wounds and persisting insecurities into the dance.

Sensitivity gaps can abound! The challenge isn't to get rid of those gaps, for they may never fully go away. Rather, the challenge – the opportunity – is to bridge those gaps when they arise, to maintain loving connection even when both of you are afraid and worried sometimes about two completely different things.

When couples fight, men tend to fear their freedom being constrained, even just their freedom to think whatever they want. Women tend to fear being abandoned, even if only emotionally. (*This is clearly not the rule for everyone)

Which perpetuates a nasty cycle: Man perceives a woman's upset to be a constraint on what he can and can't do; Woman then experiences that man's arguing for his freedom as emotionally abandoning; which makes her more upset; which makes him fight ever harder for his freedom, even if that just be from her growing upset. Wash. Rinse. Repeat. Breakup. This cycle contributes to the "Crisis of Connection" I often write about.

The essential key to relationship success is learning how to *connect in the moment*. To create connection, we must be able to suspend our own logical conclusions, at least for a moment. It requires us to connect with our own hearts, feel our own feelings, whenever the sensitivity gap shows up.

So long as you and your partner are committed to growing – me and my partner are – then your relationship will be the most powerful transformational container for your growth. Sometimes growing will be downright fucking painful. But often to grow, you only need stay in the room and feel what is there to be felt, even if what you feel is agonizing. You might be surprised what arises underneath your judgments and conclusions.

Silvy and I still regularly discover old wounds at the core of our disagreements, that have nothing to do with each other: childhood abuses and neglects, past intimate betrayals, even ancestral wounds and tragedies we somehow carry in our own bodies.

We once believed these wounds arising meant we must not be right for each other. We were wrong. It means we finally found someone with whom we feel "safe enough" to let our guard down, and all those unhealed wounds we'd both kept long hidden away from untrusted hearts are now free to show their gargoyle faces. Our work now isn't to shove them back down again where they'll only lurk in our shadows and silently sabotage our hearts' deepest desires.

Our work now is to feel everything – and keep our hearts open to bigger possibilities for our life together that our single-self-survival-minded brains can't possibly come up with if they only accept what they already believe.

Sometimes we must choose to end a relationship. When you're ready to grow and your partner refuses to join you. Or you no longer share the same purpose for the relationship. Or boundaries have been so blatantly violated you don't feel safe – whether mentally, emotionally, or physically – to continue.

Sometimes we must choose to simply not accept our conclusions, and instead, perhaps, seek help outside our own brains to see what we cannot (yet) see.

Silvy and I continue to choose this second way together. To feel all that we feel beneath our upsets. To not believe every conclusion we make, but instead be willing to see what we cannot yet see. We're now four years into the most exquisite intimate relationship either of us has ever known. That choice has made all the difference.

EPILOGUE

YOU'RE READY FOR ALL OF HER, YOU'RE A GODDAMN WARRIOR

My dear proud brother, I know why you've always struggled to truly, fully love every woman you've ever wanted to truly, fully love.

I know why every romance you ever indulged in for more than a sweet, fleeting moment soon threatened to overwhelm you.

I know why you still sometimes feel the urge to run from the burdens of relationship towards the promise of freedom in quiet, faraway hills where no woman will ever find—and why you may be tempted to stay there forever.

I also know why you always return to Her … and why you always will.

Because you're not just merely a man; you're a goddamn Warrior. *For Love.*

Deep in the marrow of your masculine core, you know you didn't come here to play safe and pass time simply scoring goals and notches on your bed post or making money and fragile monuments to your pride.

Hell no.

You came here to throw down with life, to get bloody and muddy earth all over your soul as you charge gallantly each day beyond the edges of your hard-earned comfort zone.

You are wise, ancient stardust sculpted into mighty earth come alive. You are a volcano with hot molten heart at your core, risen to offer your authentic Love even in the face of forces that would overwhelm lesser men.

I know what's been asked of you in this lifetime isn't easy.

But if you're ready to claim your birthright as a King amongst

Kings, a heart-centered warrior-protector of the planet and all things true and good and beautiful, then it's time you learn how to love a wild woman in her deliciously untamable fullness.

And you are ready to love all of her, because you're a goddamn warrior.

I know your fathers and brothers and schoolyard playmates warned you to be wary of her. Through stern faces masking an ignorance they dare not confess, they insisted that the emotions and tears and unpredictable extremes of a feminine heart have no place in the productive, rational world of a "real man."

Either flee or subdue the unpredictable heart of any woman in your midst, they cautioned, lest her raw power snap all your straight lines, ruin your portfolio and mercilessly break your fragile grip on sanity.

But you don't buy that bullshit anymore.

Oh, I know you still tremble at the thought of her fiery Kali spirit unleashed like a hurricane in your world. You've been gutted and wrecked countless times by awful perversions of love. Too many women in their own fear and immaturity have assigned you the mission impossible task of making them happy and then tried to hang you when you failed.

Your psyche has been so badly burnt you can barely imagine anymore the woman who would inspire your devotion.

Fortunately, my good man, all that agony was just warrior bootcamp.

Every chaotic, heart-wrenching love affair only served to bleed out the immature and wounded parts of you that would otherwise overthrow your Kingly heart.

You didn't know it, but life has been preparing you for what's about to happen: Your unconditional surrender to a dazzling love that will sweep through you like a wildfire at dawn.

When she arrives, this love will finally teach you how to breathe through your heart down your spine and into your balls so you can stand full and courageous before the fire-breathing dragons life will never stop sending at you.

Naturally, your woman will train you with your own dragons, the ones still lurking in your shadows. She will know exactly where to find them and which spells turn them against you. She'll delight in casting those spells, too, but only because she revels in watching you with hungry, primal eyes claim your mastery.

For that's her greatest gift to you: Mastery in devotion to Love.

She will send those dragons after you whenever she doubts your commitment – not your commitment to her little tyrant ego's selfish demands. No, she's done her deep inner work enough to know we didn't come to serve that scavenger dog.

It's your commitment to love's will that she wants to trust deeply. That's the only way she'll know you won't abandon her and run for the hills when her own dragons get loose and try to set your hair on fire.

Oh, it's gonna be spectacular, my brother!

For this journey of devotion is your awakening to the massive truth of who you already are: Love, itself!

So give up once and for all using women's healing energy to fill the goddess-size hole that ages of patriarchy ripped out of your heart.

Stop trying to shrink women into cute, manageable little pets who ask so little of you, and who you can easily love and accept. That just turns them into "not enough" for your daring soul, anyway.

You don't need some passive sex-toy with an off-switch that you keep in the closet. You need a spirited sorceress singing shaman songs beside you as you sharpen your sword for battle, because you're a goddamn warrior, after all.

You're ready for the sacred quest to love all of her.

She will serve you well on this journey, for this one likes to run with the wild things. She will shine like bright starlight in your eyes and dance like fire to light your way home to your true self.

But it's only her courage to offer you the fullness of her feminine soul, from her rage to her radiance, that will truly help you navigate deeper into the mystical realms of devotion. No timid woman will ever do for a true warrior.

Your muse is looking for you, my brother, and she'll probably show up all smiley and sweet-scented. But make no mistake:

She will be the best teacher of unconditional love you have ever known.

I suggest you leave your armor behind for this quest. Protecting yourself will only keep away what you most deeply desire, anyway. Learning to love all of her will require you leave everything behind, actually, except your own authentic heart.

For she's aching for nothing less than your true authentic heart to step up and boldly claim the untold treasures buried deep within her own.

ABOUT THE AUTHOR

A former US Air Force Captain, Bryan Reeves is now an internationally renowned Author, Blogger, and Life/Relationship Coach. Since starting his blog in 2009, his articles have been read by over 50 million people in every country on the planet (except possibly North Korea) and been translated into dozens of languages.

With a Masters Degree in Human Relations – and decades of experience studying (and burning in) the transformational fires of intimate relationship – Bryan coaches men, women and couples in creating thriving lives and relationships.

He has served on the Executive Council for the Global Alliance for Transformational Entertainment (GATE) and has helped produce hundreds of spirituality and mindfulness events featuring worldwide luminaries like Marianne Williamson, Rev. Michael Beckwith, Deepak Chopra, The Oracle of Tibet, Don Miguel Ruiz, Neale Donald Walsch and many others.

He's been a regular blog contributor to The Good Men Project, Thought Catalog, and is the author of three books, including <u>Tell The Truth, Let The Peace Fall Where It May</u>. Find Bryan on Facebook (@BryanReevesOfficial), Instagram (@BryanReevesInsight) and his website (www.BryanReeves.com).

Made in the USA
Middletown, DE
11 July 2021